IT SEEMED LIKE A GOOD IDEA...

IT SEEMED LIKE A GOOD IDEA...

A Compendium of Great Historical Fiascoes

EDITED BY

WILLIAM R. FORSTCHEN and BILL FAWCETT

Quill

An Imprint of HarperCollinsPublishers

HarperCollins books may be purchased for educational, business, or sales promotional use. For information please write: HarperCollins Publishers Inc., 10 East 53rd Street, New York, New York 10022-5299.

First Post Road Printing: February 2000
Reprinted in Quill: June 2000

Designed by Kellan Peck

Library of Congress Cataloging-in-Publication Data
    It seemed like a good idea—: a compendium of great historical fiascoes/
edited by William R. Forstchen and Bill Fawcett.
      p. cm.
    "An Avon Book."
    Includes index.
    ISBN: 0-380-80771-8
    1. History—Miscellanea.   2. History—Erros, inventions, etc.
1. Forstchen, William R. II. Fawcett, Bill.
D10.I88 2000
902—dc21   99-053525

01 02 03 04 RRD 10 9 8 7 6 5 4

Special thanks to Jody Lynn Nye and
Brian Thomsen for their contributions.
Thanks also to Stephen S. Power
for his patience and understanding.

Contents

Introduction

So many bad decisions, so few pages. When one studies history and has the advantage of 20/20 hindsight you are constantly amazed at the decisions made by otherwise very intelligent leaders. Stalin helped train the German Panzer Corps, Napoleon turned away Robert Fulton and his paddlewheelers, and the Kaiser's own spies actually smuggled Lenin into Russia to start his Bolshevik revolution. There are so many examples of seemingly irrational decisions that one sometimes has to wonder about the sanity of the decision maker and the many other equally possible courses history might have taken.

To be included in this volume the decisions had to meet a few qualifications. First they had to be seriously and unquestionably bad. Further, the decision had to be of some importance, affecting thousands, if not millions, of people. Generally we avoided using decisions made in the heat of battle. Too many can be explained by poor generalship or limited intelligence. Finally the decision, given the information at hand and the way things were done at the time, had to seem like a good idea, even the best of all possible options, but for some small fault in logic or unconsidered possible circumstance that would prove in the end catastrophic.

So enjoy a look at history's follies and feel superior to some of the past's greatest leaders. But occasionally stop and ask yourself which of the decisions being made today, the ones that seem our leaders' most rational, will be included in the 2099 edition of this book.

Bill Fawcett

IT SEEMED LIKE A GOOD IDEA...

A Bad Way to Take a Walk

The Death of Philip of Macedon
4th Century B.C. Macedonia

by William R. Forstchen

Throughout most of his reign Philip of Macedon suffered from bad press and a serious inferiority complex. Though he had built his kingdom into the preeminent power of the Greek world, his far more cultured neighbors to the south, Corinth, Athens, and Sparta, still viewed him and his followers as crude mountain-dwelling barbarians. His own personal history and appearance didn't aid his acceptance by the upper crust. He was first and foremost a military leader who took armies into battle personally. As a result he had suffered a score of wounds. The two most grievous blows had been the loss of an eye and a spear thrust into his thigh. Neither wound had healed properly and both continued to ooze. The leg in particular emitted a horrible smell. It was also rumored that he had committed the heinous crime of matricide in clawing his way to the throne.

His personal life was equally scandalous. His first

wife was a priestess of Dionysius, in modern terminology,
a temple prostitute. At that time the practice was far more
accepted and she did claim the distinction of being the
daughter of a minor king. The real scandal was their very
public falling out. She had borne Philip a son, the legendary Alexander, and then proclaimed openly that Philip
was not the father; rather it was the god Zeus, who had
visited her bedchamber in the incarnation of a snake.
Modern political and sexual scandals pale in comparison
to the dynamics played out in the royal household in the
capital city of Pella. Philip was proclaimed a cuckold by
his wife—she was known to hang around with snakes—
and the king became notorious for his desire to sleep with
anyone who was willing, male or female.

His interactions with Alexander could be described as
a love-hate relationship. On one hand, there seemed to be
moments of genuine affection between the two. Philip did
everything possible to groom him for command, retaining
the most famous scholar of the age, Aristotle, to serve as
the boy's tutor, and he craved Alexander's acceptance by
the high-browed Greeks. For his part, young Alexander,
in his first major battle, threw his own life on the line in
order to save his father who had been surrounded and
was on the point of being overcome. Alexander literally
placed his own body between his father and the enemy
spears.

And on the other hand hatred flared as well, especially as the boy entered early manhood. The bitterness
between the boy's mother and the king simmered for
years, and boiled over when Philip took a new wife, a
girl the same age as Alexander. At the wedding feast one
of Philip's drinking buddies toasted the new marriage and
the chance to produce a legitimate heir to the throne. As

a result father and son came to blows, and on the same night Alexander and his mother fled the city, a wise move since the king might very well have had both slain in his drunken rage. For over a year civil war ensued between father and his wife and son. A truce was finally declared and the two were allowed to return.

Meanwhile, Philip's dream of bringing all of Greece to heel was at last coming to pass. At the legendary battle of Chaeronea, fought in 338 B.C., Philip defeated a combined Athenian-Theban army nearly twice his size; and the following year, at Corinth, the Corinthian League was proclaimed, an alliance of all of Greece under the aegis of Philip. Though not accepted as a social equal, the strength of his army had created him supreme warlord of all the Greeks, ready to embark on a campaign into Asia against the Persian Empire.

Alexander was the only fly in the ointment. Sent by the Macedonian king to serve as ambassador, the young Alexander had become an instant celebrity, touring Greece like a triumphal hero. The contrast between father and son was remarkable. Here was not a grizzled warrior, smelling of decaying wounds, aged from drink and sexual excess; many proclaimed that the young Alexander seemed like an earthly manifestation of a god, brilliant, witty, good-natured, physically strong and agile, stunningly handsome, the true Greek ideal of perfection. Word of Alexander's successful tour came back to Philip and caused even more unrest. The old king had led the armies and won the battles, yet it was the young upstart who seemed to be taking all the glory. Furthermore, the dark, unsettling rumors, first spread by his first wife, Olympias, were now being voiced openly: that Alexander had in his veins not the blood of Philip but rather the blood of a god.

In preparation for the campaign into Persia, a religious festival and games were to be held in Pella. As king, Philip was also chief priest, and it was his responsibility to march in procession to the temple and then to the arena to start the festivities. Representatives of all the Greek city-states would be present, many of them traveling to Pella for the first time. The city went all out in preparation, for Pella was no longer a rude barbarian capital, but must now prove itself the new heart of Greek civilization and culture.

Adding additional tension to the festival were Philip's new wife and his newborn son. Philip's old drinking buddies and the family of his new wife started to openly whisper that here at last was a true heir untainted by rumors of illegitimacy. There was another undercurrent persisting as well. An old male lover of Philip, a member of his personal guard, had had a falling out with a rival for Philip's attention. This rival had recently been killed in a skirmish and his dying wish was that his competitor should somehow be humiliated. The dead rival's wishes were carried out: Philip's old lover was invited to a party, bound, then tossed out into the street to be abused by servants and slaves. When he went to Philip to complain and demand justice, Philip took the entire incident as an uproarious joke and laughed the young man out of court for being unable to defend himself. These various currents, plots and counterplots now came to a head.

Unfortunately, at this moment Philip seized on what he considered to be an excellent idea. Tired of the gibes about his appearance, his predilections, and his tyrannical behavior, Philip settled on the idea of marching in the procession in the Greek manner . . . without any armed escorts. Ever fearful of being classified as tyrants, the rulers of most Greek city-states were expected to mingle freely on the streets and at public and private functions like any other citizens; alone, unafraid, without weapons and, most of all, without guards. For only a hated king or dictator needed such men for his protection.

Thus Philip, on the morning of the festival, decked himself out in his finest robes, stepped to the front of the parade and started off alone, limping along, waving, acknowledging the cheers of the crowd. It was a grand gesture, undoubtedly drawing positive comment from foreign observers . . . and it cost him his life. As he stepped into the tunnel leading into the arena he was suddenly surprised by his old jilted lover, who drew a dagger and plunged it into Philip's chest. Philip staggered out into the arena and collapsed in a pool of blood.

The hapless assassin was himself dead within seconds, run down by several of Alexander's friends and cut apart. Within hours, the new wife met her own fate. The bitter ex-wife, Olympias, cornered her, pointed out that suicide was better than a far more painful execution, and oversaw the termination of the young girl and her baby. By the end of the day, Alexander's hold on the throne was secure.

Conspiracy? The historians of the period, writing during the reign of the great Alexander, absolved him of guilt, leaving the case against Olympias somewhat more open. At least Philip had made his point in his quest for social acceptance; he had died like a true Greek, without any bodyguards around to help.

DIVIDE AND CONQUER

The Twin Consulship and Hannibal
219 B.C. Rome

by William R. Forstchen

In the early days of the Republic, the Romans saw clearly the contract that existed between a people and their government. By its very nature a government, no matter how well designed, will always move to usurp the liberties of its citizens, if for no other reason than the benign belief that government knows best. To insure social order, however, a government must be given certain powers, the surrendering of liberties for the greater good of all. The Romans, looking at their executive office, feared that one strong man, holding such a position, and especially as commander in chief in time of war, could easily set himself up as dictator. Thus the Roman system of electing two Consuls to serve for a year.

This seemed a practical solution, because full agreement had to be made by both in order for anything to get done. The practice was that in time of war one Consul would be recognized as the "war consul." This man would go into the field with the armies and take direct command of the troops, while the other consul stayed in Rome and ran the government. The latter also maintained direct control over the local guard and troops around Rome, insuring a counterbalance in the event the consul with the army got any meglomaniacal ideas while away at war. The one problem was that the division of labor between the two consuls was based upon a mutual decision by the two men and was not an assigned position. To the Romans this was an excellent idea. Even if a procoup faction rose up in the Senate, it was impossible for them to appoint their consul to run the army in time of war. The other consul could always block this. Now, if such an impasse should occur, the accepted practice was that *both* consuls took the field with the army and then had command on alternating days. The thinking was, better a divided command than a lone commander with dictatorship on his mind.

The system had been in place for years with few problems. The tendency was simply to divide the rule between war and home, which went successfully for many years. Rome, in fact, had emerged as the dominant power on the Italian peninsula and, by the middle of the third century B.C., had defeated the great maritime power of Carthage in the first of three wars. The defeat of Carthage in 241 B.C. left Carthage eager for a rematch. In 219 B.C. a Carthaginian army under Hannibal launched an offensive out of Spain. Within two years this army had bested the Romans in several encounters, forced a passage over the Alps, and annihilated a Roman army of 40,000 men on the shore of Lake Trasimene, less than a week's march from the gates of Rome.

Panic ensued, with fear that Hannibal would soon be

there. A brief delay was gained by the skillful Roman tactician Quintus Fabius fighting a brilliant series of rear-guard actions. By employing scorched-earth tactics he denied Hannibal much-needed supplies, raided the rear of the Carthaginian lines, and in general fought an irregular war. This was atypical of the Romans, who tended to think in direct offensive terms, and for his troubles Fabius, whose brilliant system of warfare would be forever known as "Fabian Tactics," was forced out of power.

Rome now appointed two new consuls for the year 216 B.C., Lucius Aemilius Paulus, and Gaius Terentius Varro. Paulus, the elder of the two, was skilled in battle, noted for his caution and professional skill. Varro was the exact opposite; excitable, impatient with the counsel of others, and eager for glory.

During the year which Fabius had won for Rome, a massive mobilization drive had taken place; Rome had managed to create and train a new army of over eighty thousand men. Though not yet battle tested, the ranks were sprinkled with old veterans of the last war and survivors of earlier campaigns. It was felt that with this overwhelming force, Hannibal, who was now maneuvering in the south of Italy, could be brought to bay and destroyed.

The division of the excutive branch now caused a problem with who would take the field and who would stay home. The good sense which had usually prevailed didn't work out this time. Paulus had the experience and was the natural choice for field commander. He was the only one who realized the threat Hannibal posed. This was not an opponent who had won by simple dumb luck. Even if he was brought to battle on unfavorable ground and heavily outnumbered, still he would be a hard foe to beat.

Varro disagreed violently. He thought he was just as capable as Paulus and furthermore, that Paulus should stay home and command the reserves. He argued that the old man was too cautious for this kind of warfare, and that what Rome needed was a swift and aggressive campaign of attack using their now vastly superior numbers. Varro wanted to send Hannibal's head back to Carthage and to let them know that Varro and the rest of the Roman army were coming to finish the war off once and for all.

There was no way Varro was going to let Paulus get the glory from an easy win, and absolutely no way that Paulus would give Varro free rein over the lives of 80,000 men. Finally they decided both would go and divide the command.

So in the summer of 216 B.C. the largest army Rome had ever fielded up to this time set off southward. Hannibal was waiting. As they got closer to the enemy, a bit of the bluster went out of Varro. Perhaps it was the conversations with Paulus, perhaps it was a dawning realization that running an army, and an entire war, involved more than just pointing and screaming charge. And as they approached the area controlled by Hannibal, Varro actually started to display a bit of caution. On days when he was in command, he tended to listen to what Paulus had to say about the day's maneuvers. Paulus realized that they did have the advantage in numbers. The trick was to bring Hannibal to battle on ground where those numbers would tell, where there were secured lines of retreat if something should go wrong, and where Hannibal's every response could be anticipated.

But the Romans were not ready for the move that followed. Swinging in behind them, Hannibal pulled a forced night march, falling on a Roman supply depot near the city of Cannae. After seizing the depot, he moved across a nearby river and then *put his back to the river*. He timed the maneuver to coincide with Varro's day in command.

It was brilliant in its execution. The loss of the depot most certainly wounded the pride of the Romans and could be reported as well as a failure of command, a failure which happened on a day and evening when Paulus was in command. Surveying the Carthaginian position, Varro was suddenly full of aggressive vigor. He now had Hannibal just where *he* wanted him, believing the arrogant Carthaginian general had blundered. Once his position was broken, his army would have nowhere to retreat and would be driven into the river or slaughtered. Varro ordered a full deployment of the army and made preparations for attack.

Paulus was appalled. He argued for caution. Hannibal was no fool. The seizure of the depot was designed to prick at their pride. Wasn't it obvious that Hannibal had chosen his position with the full intent of making it look vulnerable? The opposite must be true. He wanted the Romans to attack and would spring some sort of trap once battle was joined.

Varro would have nothing of Paulus' argument. He was just being a cautious old man, Varro sneered. This was a job for an aggressive, vigorous officer, not one who saw monsters hiding behind every tree and was afraid of his own shadow. Besides, today is my day to command, Varro declared, and the order of the day is . . . attack.

Perhaps Paulus should have just killed him then and there, but the Romans are people of law, and whether the consul of the day was a genius or a fool, the law was on his side when it came to who had the power at the moment.

So Varro led his army to the attack. For the first couple of hours all seemed to be going well. The center of the Carthaginian line began to crumble under the superior weight of the Roman attack. Finally the Romans had pressed almost to the river, Hannibal's formation curving like a bow. All that held were the troops anchored to either flank. Varro ordered every man into the assault so that the Romans were compressed into a huge seething mass, a human battering ram crashing into the center, relying now on sheer weight to break it.

Hannibal then gave the command to the troops on his wings who had hardly been engaged. They pivoted inward while heavy Carthaginian cavalry swung around behind the Roman lines and charged their rear as well. Within minutes the Roman army was surrounded and assaulted on all sides.

Panic ignited and the entire army disintegrated into a trapped and terrified mob. Tens of thousands were killed by their own comrades, crushed and trampled to death, or cut to pieces as men tried to slash their way clear.

By the end of the day nearly seventy thousand Romans were dead or captured. The good idea of dividing command had sent the Roman army to its doom. Ironically, the cause of it all got clear away. Varro and a few thousand men managed to hack their way out of the trap and escape back to Rome, though they were all banished for their failure. As for Paulus . . . his good advice gave him a grave on the field of Cannae. The war would drag on for another fourteen years.

STAB AT STABILITY

Death to the Tyrant, Long Live the Emperor
10 B.C. Rome

By Bill Fawcett

Rome under Julius Caesar was the center of an empire grown rich and powerful with the spoils of war. Where centuries before members of the hereditary patrician class had lived on and even farmed the lands they held, the rich senators of Rome now used slaves to work their vast estates. The free citizens of the empire were being marginalized, their farms couldn't compete with the more-efficient estates and their crafts could not compete with the production from slave factories.

The city of Rome itself had grown from a few hundred thousand residents to over two million. Feeding this mass of humanity was already proving to be a burden on the treasury and the merchant marine. The need for grain to feed the city's residents would be one of the motivating factors in their taking over Egypt and settling in the frontier of Roman Panoria, today known as the Balkans, both good sources of grain. Surging, hungry, and teeming

Rome demanded much of those who ruled her. Like all governments, the bureaucracy had taken on a life of its own. Corruption was rampant on all levels, often encouraged or controlled by the rich senatorial families who were supposed to be controlling it. Legions were being manned by fewer Italians and more citizens of the newly conquered lands. Unrest was rife; even fire fighting was a problem. Rome was still a city of wooden buildings, often several stories high. Fire fighting was vital to city safety, but like much of the government, it had become corrupt. Large areas were licensed for exorbitant fees to private companies. These in turn negotiated with each building's owner to protect or attempt to save their building if a fire occurred. Too often these companies would arrive and then, as the building burned, negotiate a further "bonus" for fighting the fire.

Politics, too, had gone from rough-and-tumble to brutally cutthroat. Factions controlled private mobs, and even the army was flexing its muscle independently. To keep the army at bay, the Senate had long had a law that forbade any military commander from bringing his army closer to the capital than the Rubicon River without the permission of the Senate . . . which it never gave. Several generals had threatened and one had even led his army over the legal line of the Rubicon River, and that one, Julius Caesar, had also gained the support of most of the plebians, the general citizenry of Rome. But other leaders, such as Lepidus, had their own legions; and one, Crassus, headed a group of men who controlled much of the wealth of the empire. Assassinations were common just below the level of the highly visible leaders, and the Senate, which once had the final word on everything, was quickly losing control.

The senators, all heads of rich families and thriving businesses, had to make a decision. More democracy would mean control by the mob. It was inevitable, that the plebians would move to better their lot at the expense of the rich elite. On the other hand were the leaders such as Caesar, who had a power base, wealth, and the ability to control the mob. This meant giving up virtually all of their authority to one of these leaders; the trade-off being that the stability this would buy could guarantee their continued financial and social positions. Or the Senate could, as some of its members advised, stand by tradition and try to maintain control of the empire. But the situation as it stood meant that, in any case, the Senate had no real power base and would soon be pushed aside by the contending factions.

So the senators met and took what was probably the line of least resistance. Julius Caesar was already First Consul, first among equals. He came from one of their own patrician families, and he had an army, proven in the Gallic Wars, at his back. If the Senate was going to appoint a strong man to control the empire, he was the obvious choice. Better to have Julius Caesar in control, guaranteeing stability, than to risk losing everything. The appointment of Julius Caesar as First Consul for Life would, they thought, ensure peace and prosperity, at least for themselves.

So, in a time of peace, but of crisis, the patrician families of Rome voted for a dictator. Julius Caesar knew what a departure this was and three times, falsely acknowledging a reluctance to change the very heart of the Roman system, he refused the title he had worked so hard to gain. Ultimately he accepted and everyone in the Senate was relieved, except for a few traditionalists who felt the entire system had been betrayed. These men spoke of the rights of all Romans and the sacred duty of the Senate to rule, and like Sam Adams and our own Founding Fathers in 1776, they decided to take matters into their own hands.

There is no record of any augury warning Caeser in the historical records, and so on the Ides of March, he approached the Senate Chamber to announce a number of laws for which he wanted pro forma approval. In a short time Julius Caesar had taken absolute control of all of the Roman Empire, and the next years he had defeated Pompey and other potential military competitors. Peace and stability did return briefly, but at the cost of a figure-head Senate and through the founding of the Imperial Roman system.

What happened next is well recorded and has been immortalized, inaccurately, by Shakespeare. The tradition-alists, in an attempt to force the Senate to accept its re-sponsibilities, and to undo the damage they saw from Caesar's appointment, assassinated the First Consul.

So now we have two decisions that seemed to be the best that could be made, first to appoint Julius Caesar effectively dictator for life, and second to reverse that de-cision by ending that life. As to the success of the first, Caesar had to defeat his enemies to consolidate his power, which led to a series of battles between legions, the first such on any scale in history. Once Caesar was killed the weakened Senate had no choice but to turn to other strong leaders to maintain the order they had sold their power for, and the next years were ones of near-constant internal warfare. First two sets of three leaders competed. Then, when Augustus, Anthony, and Crassus, won they turned on each other. The cost in men and wealth was incredible.

When the remaining three Consuls turned on each other, more civil war followed. Ultimately Augustus Caesar emerged the victor and there was peace, nearly a hundred years of peace, at the cost of Imperial and totally arbitrary rule by a single man. But, by the end of these internal battles, Rome had ceased to be an expansionist power. Its days of sweeping conquests were past. Eventually the quality of the emperors waned, and within two hundred years they seemed to arrive and leave with the tides. All stability was lost. The Senate lost its relevance and became a facade. For a short period of stability the empire paid with dictatorial rule and the occasional mad emperor, like Caligula.

The much maligned Brutus and his faction of assassins failed even more miserably in the name of senatorial power. Until its fall almost five centuries later, not a single emperor even felt the need to regularly consult the Senate, much less be constrained by its dictates. Caligula probably said it best when he appointed his horse to that once august body.

But at the time, the election of Caesar, even his assassination, certainly seemed to be the right idea.

SINS OF THE SISTER

The Personal Loss of an Entire Continent
1001 A.D. Scandinavia

By Bill Fawcett

In the eleventh century the Viking nations were at the peak of their power. Their laws were well developed, their reputation for ferocity well established, and their rulers among the richest and most powerful in the world. One of the greatest prides of Byzantium was the emperor's Varangian guard, consisting entirely of Viking warriors recruited from Russia and other Scandinavian settlements. And their longships held sway on coasts and rivers from Dublin to Kiev.

But surprisingly, they didn't settle in North America even though they had the earliest opportunity of all the European peoples. The Viking greed for land was almost as strong as their desire for gold, and the verdent "Vinland" coast of Nova Scotia, would have been a great prize. Also it has better weather than Iceland and Greenland, both successfully settled by the Vikings, as well as their homeland, Norway, whose soil is poor and whose weather is at best dismal. Resistance by the natives didn't hinder settlement. While the Vikings lacked the technical edge over the native Indians that the rifle would give America's European settlers, their armor and steel weaponry did give them a distinct advantage. Nor did distance. It is half as far from Greenland to the North American coast as it is from Norway to Iceland, or Iceland to Greenland. You can stand in Nova Scotia, even today, and see cloud effects on the distant horizon that are generated by the higher Greenland peaks. So why didn't one of the most expansionist and dynamic peoples of Europe ever take a continent ripe for the plucking?

The answer lies in the dark history of two of the most famous men in Viking history, Eric the Red, or Bloody, and one of his progeny, Leif Ericson.

Although Vikings were infamous for raping and pillaging, Eric the Red was too violent even for them. First he was banished to Iceland, where Leif was born, from Norway because he murdered an unarmed neighbor over what should have been a minor dispute. Once he settled on Iceland, he got into another argument which resulted in his killing one of the longtime residents. There being nowhere known at that time to further banish him, Eric was ordered to move to the western edge of Iceland where there were few neighbors. That didn't work either, as a few years later, in 982, Eric got into another dispute and killed yet again, earning his sobriquet. Now Eric was ordered off Iceland. But the murderer also had his charms. He gathered about him a group of discontented or bored Vikings, they built several new longships, and then they sailed west.

Eric and his followers sailed for about five hundred miles before sighting land. This was what we today call

Greenland, a euphemistic name Eric gave the ice-packed region to attract settlers. Eric and his comrades sailed back to Iceland and enticed a few hundred Viking families to establish a colony there. Although the weather was lousy and the soil rocky, the former was tolerable because the latter was free, and so the colony of perhaps 500 struggled on under the de facto leadership of Eric.

In 1001 Eric's son Leif was hit by the wanderlust that seemed to inspire all Vikings of that era. But he had a definite idea as to where to go. Signs and even sightings told of another island further west. His father was still ruler of Greenland and this helped Leif gather a crew and sail in search of this new land. After a surprisingly short sail they arrived on the coast of Nova Scotia. Like his father, Leif knew the importance of a good name for attracting settlers, so he called it Vinland, though the name does not really have anything to do with grapes, but translates more as "fertile" or "friendly" land. He then sailed back to Greenland, now a thriving community of about 1500, to announce his discovery, recruit settlers, and do on Vinland what his father had done on Greenland.

But fate intervened. Eric the Red died, leaving his throne to Leif. It appears he ruled well and the colony grew under his leadership, but the next few years kept Leif too busy to exploit Vinland. This task fell to his sister, Freydis, as a result.

Her first expedition marks the first real interaction between the local Indians and the Vikings. When it became apparent that the Vikings were building stone houses and planned to stay, the natives practiced a little local zoning control. They banded together and drove the fifty or so Vikings back to their ships. Freydis was the heroine in their losing effort, turning on the pursuing Indians and, by sheer ferocity, driving them back until the ships could be loaded safely.

A few years later Freydis led a larger group to the same spot. This time they were better armed and more numerous, but the colony got off to a bad start. It seems that Freydis' ship wasn't the first to arrive. When she landed, the house she had planned to claim was already occupied by two brothers and their families. In the tradition of her father, Eric the Bloody, Freydis objected. No one felt the need to intervene when she killed both brothers, but they drew the line at being ordered to slaughter their wives and children as well. In a fit of rage Freydis grabbed a war ax and did the job herself.

Later that year the colonists returned to winter in Greenland. An effort was made to hush up the slaughter of the two families, but someone talked. This put Leif in a very awkward position. His sister had killed, without cause, women and children he was responsible for protecting. By rights he should have killed the murderer, but executing one's sister was just as great a breach of Viking law. Finally, bitterly and forcefully, Leif reached a compromise: he ordered his sister banished and he banned all travel to Vinland. Perhaps he hoped to have the story fade from memory if Vinland was no longer inhabited, and so allow him to bring his sister back. More likely he was so bitter over the entire fiasco that he simply didn't want to ever be again reminded of it or the scene of the murders.

The ban stuck. Even after Leif's death, a series of poor harvests and severe winters meant that there was little consideration for expanding the colony west to North America. Instead most of the residents conceded the inevitable and returned east to Iceland. A few held out, but two hundred and fifty years later Greenland was again uninhabited by Europeans. During all this time, because of a murder in the family, Leif's ban on settling Vinland was honored. As a result, the most dynamic race of that era lost the chance to dominate North America. How different the world would be today if Eric's son had not banned all travel to the land of his sister's disgrace, but at the time it seemed like the right thing to do.

THERE'S NOTHING WORSE THAN AN IDEALISTIC WAR

The Crusades in the Middle East
1095 Jerusalem

By William R. Forstchen

It was started over the most noble of ideals, the liberation of a holy land supposedly possessed by an infidel barbarian horde, and it triggered a millennium of strife and created a tinderbox that to this very day threatens to explode with more violence. But behind the idealism, there were more pragmatic and commercial reasons. Tourists by the thousands flocked there every year out of Europe, generating brisk and flourishing business. In addition to the Europeans, the Arabs, who had taken the Holy Land from the Byzantine Empire in the seventh century, viewed the region as equally sacred, with Jerusalem the third most sacred city after Medina and Mecca.

In the eleventh century the situation heated up somewhat when the Seljuk Turks, who embraced a more fundamentalist view, swept into the area. There were now occasional incidents of tourists getting mugged, being ripped off by sudden new taxes, having their mules hijacked, and falling victim to foul play. Naturally, reports of this filtered back into Europe, the telling and retelling greatly magnifying the indignities, though one cannot help but wonder how a boatload of Moslem tourists would have been treated if they had landed in eleventh century Paris or London.

The ever increasing threat to the city of Constantinople added to the tension. In 1072, the year prior to the fall of Jerusalem to the Seljuks, the Byzantine army had gone down in a disastrous defeat at the Battle of Manzikert. For the next twenty years the Turks pressed their advantage in Anatolia (now known as Turkey), and it now appeared as if the city itself might fall against a determined assault.

The Byzantine emperors sent a series of desperate appeals to the West, directing them in particular to the pope. Relationships between the papacy and the Byzantine emperors had been strained for hundreds of years, the key issue being whether the emperor must acknowledge the supremacy of the pope. The threat of the Seljuk advances pushed the emperor into a corner and a willingness to compromise. He did add the telling argument, which would later prove true, that if Constantinople fell, the back door to Europe would be open and soon central Europe would be the battleground.

Finally, in 1095, Pope Urban II stirred himself to action, motivated by several factors. He recognized the Byzantine argument, that their city was in fact the front line for the defense of Europe, was a valid one. Secondly he knew that there were simply too many armored knights wandering about, trained for only one thing, violence. Europe of the eleventh century bore, in some ways, a striking resemblance to the armed gangs that terrorize our urban environments today, and far too many civilians were getting in the way. The pope, who hadn't been able to stop the carnage, struck upon the idea that if he couldn't keep them from slaughtering each other, maybe the answer was to turn them lose on a bunch of infidels. The killing of non-Christians in the name of God was not a sin, aggressive energies would be vented, and, best of all, the violence would happen somewhere else. Ultimately, there was the belief that freeing the Holy Land was a good idea and would actually serve the greater glory of God.

So, in 1095, Urban II gave a rousing speech, calling for a Holy War to take back the Holy Land, and unleashed forces never dreamed of.

Urban had expected the Crusade to be a small, well-organized effort of professional soldiers, not more than twenty or thirty thousand, the sheer nightmare of organizing logistical support in the eleventh century being the major constraint on the numbers. Unfortunately, within a matter of months, nearly a hundred thousand peasants under Peter the Hermit set off on their own People's Crusade. With grossly flawed logic Peter argued that since God loved the common people, surely he would grant to them the honor of liberating the Holy Land. By the time this mob entered Hungary it was starving and pillaged as it advanced. When they arrived in Constantinople, the emperor immediately ferried the peasants over to Anatolia where they were promptly massacred by the waiting Turks.

When the first crusade arrived in Constantinople in 1097 they were met by an awestruck and more than slightly frightened Emperor Alexius. They numbered upwards of a hundred thousand, a number simply far too big to manage and supply. His appeals for help had been for a small professional force that would be willing to take oaths of fealty to him and fight for his primary cause, taking back Anatolia. The Holy Land had been merely an idealistic objective, never considered attainable. Instead he was confronted with tens of thousands of brawling, unruly knights, retainers, and arrogant princes, more than one of them rivals who had been at war with the Byzantines only a couple of years before.

Needless to say he closed the gates of the city, rightfully fearing that if given a chance this mob might actually try to seize his throne. However, for their part, the Crusaders were disgusted with the Byzantines and their crafty ways. They had not come all this way merely to fight for an emperor and his personal gain. They wanted the Holy Land, and the promise of remission of all sins and a guaranteed ticket to heaven if they should die in the process. An uneasy time passed with the Greeks feeding this new army, and trying to figure out a way to hasten it along while at the same time benefitting somehow. Their idealism was already taking a back seat.

The following spring the campaign kicked off under the nominal command of the Byzantines. The following two years were a bloody, grueling advance through terrain and climate totally alien to the knights of France, Germany and England. At least two-thirds of the men died along the way from the punishing heat and combat. Finally, after nearly three years, their goal was in sight, the Holy City of the Prince of Peace, Jerusalem.

The assault began, the walls were breached, and what ensued was truly one of the worst and most bloodthirsty massacres in history, with nearly the entire population of the city put to the sword. The souls of the attackers were considered protected by the promise of immortal salvation, so the fact that over half the population of the city was Jewish and Christian did not seem to weigh too heavily upon them.

Thus ended the First Crusade, and for the next eighty years the Holy Land was divided up into Crusader States, although the skirmishing continued as well. The papal plan had actually liberated the Holy Land, but slaughtered hundreds of thousands in the process.

The monolithic endeavor only got worse. Historians like to clump events into convenient groupings, and thus we can read about a Second Crusade, a Third Crusade, etc., but it was almost a continual process. Waves of Crusaders flooded into the region for well over two hundred years. Some were motivated by genuine piety, others were sent as penance for remission of a sin, but many others came as part of the general land and loot grab unleashed by the wars.

During the twelfth century additional crusaders came out of France, and from as far away as Norway and Denmark. Many of these Norse crusaders traversed the length of Russia to get to their goal. The most famed of these subsequent rampages was the Third Crusade of the legendary King Richard the Lionhearted.

The Third Crusade actually began with a tangible goal; in 1187 Saladin, leading his own Moslem Crusade, had recaptured Jerusalem from the Christians. This affront to Western sensibilities united the kings of England, France and the Holy Roman Empire in a sacred quest, temporarily replacing their old feuds back home.

Richard fought for over half a dozen years and only once did the army even get within sight of Jerusalem—so skillful and fanatical was the defense. Finally, making the best of a bad deal, a truce was struck, granting tourist rights to the Holy City to the westerners. As Richard headed for home he was waylaid by a rival, locked up, and held for ransom. One would think that the English would have thanked the kidnapper, for the forgotten side of the legend of Richard is that since his ascension to the throne he had barely set foot in England, viewing it as nothing more than a bottomless money pouch and supplier of bodies for his noble efforts. He had bankrupted the country as a result, and his ransom sent it into even deeper financial trouble. The irony is that his brother, John got hung with all the blame for squeezing the country in order to get his brother out of jail. Richard came back home, ran the country into even deeper debt organizing a new army, then went off to attack his former ally, France, where he was promptly killed. John spent the rest of his reign trying to repair the damage, and received even more negative press.

The Crusades still continued, half a dozen more waves of attacks were carried out over the next century, of which the most infamous and disastrous was the Fourth. Starting in France, the expedition wound up in Venice looking for transport, where another "good idea" as cynical as any in history unfolded. The Venetians, remarkable for their diplomatic cunning, convinced the French army to serve as mercenaries in a personal fight to take Zara (now Zadar) back from Hungary before being transported to the Holy War. The French went along with the deal. Zara was taken back and looted, an action which resulted in the entire army being excommunicated by the pope. Things went downhill from there. The Venetians now dangled the riches of Byzantium itself before their hired army, and under the pretext of restoring a deposed relative of the Byzantine emperor, the Crusaders now stormed

Constantinople, set the city afire, massacred a fair part of the population and looted the place clean, and in passing put their own puppet on the throne. The original cause of the Crusades, to help protect Constantinople against the Turks was completely ignored, and this perfidious attack ended up hurting Europe. Eventually the old Byzantine line reestablished itself on the throne of the ancient city, but they were now merely a pale shadow of their former power and glory. The eventual decline of an empire that could trace its lineage back to the Caesars can be marked from this moment.

This fourth crusader army, rich with the spoils of war, finally wandered back home. Ten years later the pope tried again. This army tried to establish a base of operations in Egypt, which was an unusual choice, but got bogged down in the disease-ridden marshes of the Nile delta and finally gave up and went home.

More efforts were mounted. In the 1260s the Mongol invasion of the region, and a new Egyptian dynasty of slaves trained as warriors, the Mamelukes, fell upon each other creating additional problems for the Crusaders. Each side actually appealed to the Crusaders to ally with them and for a brief time it appeared as if a Mongol would be the new liberator of Jerusalem. The Mongols, however, bypassed the city and shortly afterwards withdrew.

One of the most horrid crusades was the Children's Crusade. The medieval cities of Europe were aswarm with orphaned and abandoned children, and several of them became convinced that where adults had failed children would surely succeed, for God would protect them in their march to the Holy City. By the thousands the children of Europe poured out and headed to the coast, begging and stealing along the way to stay alive. The Church did make an effort to try to dissuade them, but nothing could turn them aside in their innocent fervor. Reaching ports along the coast of Italy, the leaders negotiated with a consortium of ship owners who, in exchange for God's blessings, would provide transport to the Holy Land. The deal was struck, the children were loaded aboard, and in a fiendish display of capitalism and social engineering the entire lot of poor children was sent to North Africa and sold into slavery for a profit.

One famous crusade never even got out of France. In alliance with the king of France the pope declared a holy crusade against the Albigensian heretics in the south of that country, and gave his holy blessings to thousands of French nobles from the north. They rampaged into the Provence region, sacking Albigensian and non-Albigensian strongholds alike and seizing their land.

The crusading spirit finally simmered down in the fourteenth century as, one by one, the last of the strongholds on the coast of the Holy Land and the islands of the eastern Aegean fell to renewed waves of Mameluke and Ottoman Turkish assault. The advent of the Hundred Years War, the bitter rivalries of the Italian city-states, and the Great Plague finally ended the Crusades. The results were appalling. The Byzantine Empire was a hollowed-out wreck, hundreds of thousands had died, and Moslems saw European Christians as rapacious invaders who had to be pushed back at all costs. The good idea of a war of liberation had turned into what all wars turn into, a nasty brutish and *long* affair, made worse by religious hatred, greed, and the madness of idealism.

SAFE AND SORRY

Emperor Alexius and the Siege of Antioch
1097 The Byzantine Empire

By Bill Fawcett

A strange confluence of forces split Europe, both religiously and politically. With nine centuries worth of perspective, the division between the eastern and western halves of the Roman Empire seem obvious. At the time in the West defending the powerful Byzantine Empire wasn't even seen as important. The everyday affairs of those involved, the needs of the nobles and rulers, were of immediate concern. Even the extreme theological debate over the decisions of the Council of Nicaea, the basis for the Nicene Creed still memorized by most Roman Catholics, was considered less important than the mutual interests of all churchmen and Christians. Though the governments were divided, they still remembered their place in the greater Roman Empire, an image so strong that the title of Emperor of the Holy Roman Empire was jealously guarded by the Austrian monarchy even a thousand years later. And the Greek-speaking citizens of what we call the

Byzantine Empire called themselves Rhomaio and their empire Romania. No, it wasn't theology that split Europe into
two irretrievably separate parts; it was the caution and
seeming prudence of one of the most effective rulers to sit
on the throne in Constantinople, Alexius.

When the armies of Islam succeeded in conquering
Syria and then much of the Balkans, also known as
Roman Panoria, the loss cost the Byzantine Empire much
of its manpower and tax income. As a result the emperor
cast about for a way to add to his strength, or at least
cause the rising Islamic rulers problems. One of his many
efforts was to write the current pope in Rome for
assistance . . . in freeing the Holy Land.

Pope Urban II answered that letter on a scale far beyond anything Alexius expected, or possibly desired. It
seems that the near-constant warfare in Western Europe
was abating. This was causing thousands of petty knights
and men at arms to suddenly become unemployed and
often homeless. The effect of taking those best trained in
combat and suddenly making them indigent was a crime
wave on a level never before seen. Entire companies of
men became outlaws or simply took over areas and ex-
torted taxes from the residents. The armies of the rightful
rulers had their hands full within their borders, and there
is no money to be made for the kingdom if you are fighting inside it. The rulers were unhappy, but had no use
for the former soldiers. The people and merchants were
suffering. Even more alarming, this lawlessness was drastically lowering the tithes collected by church leaders that
were needed to maintain their lifestyles and construction
of their cathedrals.

So the pope had a problem; too many unemployed
soldiers wandering about wreaking havoc. And when he

got a letter from Alexius asking for manpower to achieve
a holy purpose, it seemed that God had provided a solution to both problems. Pope Urban began preaching a crusade to free the Holy Land. Unemployed and restless
soldiers, peasants who didn't have enough land to survive
on, and nobles anxious to find glory, or just to escape the
debt and boredom they often faced in their homes, all
flocked to a cause that guaranteed them a seat in heaven.

Where Alexius was likely expecting a few thousand
men, perhaps a few shiploads of papal troops, or a small
fleet at most, he suddenly discovered that thousands of
knights and soldiers, and their retinues, were marching
and sailing toward him and at his own invitation. The
worrisome fact was that the Western army, including rulers of lands as great as his own, would easily outnumber
the garrison he could afford to maintain in his capital.
There was the very real chance that after the Crusaders
arrived they would be able to simply take over what remained of his empire before ever facing any Islamic army.
The fact that the majority of those approaching were noto-
riously proud, very violent, and generally illiterate didn't
help either. Over a century later this is exactly what happened, when a Crusader army got as far as the capital
and then proceeded to pillage it unmercifully, a blow
from which the city never recovered. By the time it did
fall to the Turks, the population had dwindled by 60%.

The Byzantine emperor found a solution. When the
ships of the crusading army arrived, he refused to allow
them to enter the harbor until they agreed to swear allegiance to him as liege lord. This had the additional effect
of causing all of the lands they did conquer to become
part of his feudal domains. This was all well and good,
but the liege lord has responsibilities as well. Perhaps the

most important of these was the aid and protection he guaranteed. In the Western kingdoms this often took the form of making good on the ransom demanded by another knight who had captured a liegeman in battle. It was an arrangement that worked best among the smaller kingdoms of the West, where most nobles knew each other personally, even enemies. But Alexius was the emperor of Byzantium, which, while diminished from its former glory, was still a sizable kingdom. It was likely there were far more citizens in the city of Constantinople than the total of all those who were ruled from Paris at that time.

But Alexius was able to hurry his newly pledged lieges on their way, and within a few months the army had defeated one Turkish force and was besieging Antioch. The siege was a long one and the Turks had plenty of time to gather a new army. The Crusaders prevailed and entered the city, thanks in part to the timely arrival of ships of food and supplies sent by Emperor Alexius. But within a few months the Turkish army had once again put the Crusaders under siege inside the walls of Antioch. However, the Turks were unable to break through the walls, which resulted in another protracted siege. Worse yet, the Turks seemed to be mobilizing yet another force, their supply lines being short and their population several times larger than that which remained to Romania.

As would be expected in the West, the Crusaders sent word to their liege lord to come bail them out. Now Alexius basically had one army. It did double duty in guarding against invasion and protecting Constantinople, which sat uncomfortably exposed to assault. He found his newly assumed responsibilities as liege lord in conflict with those of his role as emperor. If he marched to Antioch he had to win a quick and decisive victory because, with the army gone, what remained of the empire would be defenseless. But if he marched and failed, there was no recourse, no way to recover and save anything. The Turks would overrun the million plus people he was also sworn to protect.

The decision was to follow the Roman strategy. To maintain his army as a reserve and leave the Crusaders to their own devices. He had only just become their liege lord and had to consider his empire's needs first. The Crusaders were outraged by what they viewed as a betrayal. But anger was the least of their reactions. To everyone's surprise, a month later, desperate and near starvation, the entire Crusader army sallied out of Antioch and routed the besieging force. The victory was so complete that they went on to capture numerous other cities. They were released from their oaths by Alexius' betrayal, and appointed their own kings to rule them. When these same Crusaders, now heroes and survivors, returned home to Western Europe, they spoke of nothing more than Alexius' duplicity and lack of honor.

If you were one of the citizens Alexius chose to protect, you knew he had made the right decision. Considering the weakened position of the Crusaders, it was probably the correct military decision. But by abandoning a large part of Western nobility while they were in need, and blatantly failing to fulfill his duties under an oath he had forced those nobles to swear, Alexius widened and made permanent a division between the two Europes that still remains to this day. Prudence and caution seemed like the only decision to opt for at the time, but not answering the Crusaders' plea had the effect of dividing Europe permanently. Nor did his efforts really spare his capital. The ill will and distrust this one decision created led to the eventual sack of Constantinople by another generation of Western knights raised to think of it as an enemy capital, not another part of their Christian world.

THE BURNING OF BEARDS

Shah 'Ala' ad-Din Muhammad and Genghis Khan 13th Century Khwarezm Empire

by William R. Forstchen

For 'Ala' ad-Din Muhammad the signs were troubling although his vast holding, the Khwarezm Empire, which encompassed the modern states of Iran, Pakistan, Afghanistan, and most of the new CIS nations of central Asia, was undoubtedly the wealthiest empire on earth in the early thirteenth century.

Set astride the great silk trade routes, caravans from China, India, the Middle East, Kievan Rus, and even from as far as Western Europe, all intersected at the great merchant cities of Merv, Bokhara, and Samarkand. It was said that Samarkand had a population of well over half a million, at a time when Paris and London were filthy hovels of but thirty to forty thousand. Vast pleasure gardens canopied by exotic fruit trees, cooled by sparkling fountains, and populated by courtesans from every corner of the known world were there for the pleasure of the nobility. It was a center of learning as well, for the universities and

39

libraries of all the great cities made the shah's empire the center of art, poetry, and learning for the world of Islam. Nor was it a state made soft by centuries of decadent wealth. A successful series of wars had expanded the boundaries of the empire in all directions and the shah could place an army of 500,000 in the field, nearly all of them mounted and heavily armored; this at a time when the resources of France, Germany and England were strained to the utmost to place fifty thousand men into the campaigns in the Holy Land. The Khwarzm Empire bestrode the world and from the Dnieper to the Pacific none dared to arouse its wrath.

Yet there was troubling news for the shah. Nothing truly serious but annoying, like the buzzing of a lone fly that has slipped through canopied curtains to disturb one's sleep. Far to the east, well over two thousand miles away, a new power was emerging, a barbaric kingdom of nomadic riders: unlettered, dwellers of tent cities, raiders, thieves. Word had come that, in the year 1206 by the Christian calendar, they had united together about a single war chief, declaring that he was the Great King of Kings or Perfect War Emperor, Genghis Kha Khan in their language. This khan had successfully breached the Great Wall of the Chinese and plundered their northern provinces.

A Tartar chieftain, Kushluk, had dared to rebel against this new overlord by leading a rebellion in the state of Karakitai (in what is now western China), a neighbor to the Khwarezm Empire. Playing the game that any shrewd ruler would, the Great Shah of the Khwarezm secretly gave support to this rebel, so as to keep the barbarian nomads divided against themselves. If this Kushluk should ever grow too strong himself, the shah probably resolved, he could always pay off Genghis in turn.

He should have first realized somthing was wrong when Genghis sent but two tumens, 20,000 men, under one of his brilliant generals, Chepe, up into the mountains to root the rebellion out, and Chepe annihilated his foe in a bitter six-year campaign.

Now advanced contingents of Genghis' barbarians controlled a small section of the empire's eastern border. It was not a logical route for invasions, though, because it was guarded by the Pamir mountains, a range soaring as high as 25,000 feet.

Business continued as usual. Caravans came from across the world, paying taxes as they arrived, trading with the merchants of the cities, who paid taxes as well, and all was well in the world. Messengers from this new khan would arrive on occasion, bearing some trinkets as gifts of friendship and the usual gifts were sent back in return. But a disturbing trend was noticed.

Barbarian Mongols started to arrive with the caravans as well. They proclaimed themselves to be merchants, merely moving the surplus of spoils taken in the land of the Chin, looking for profitable exchange in the bazaars of the great cities, but the shah's intelligence service was not pleased. They reported that these "merchants" were actually spies, taking note of the strength of fortifications, the location of troops, and the number of catapults lining city walls. In the language of a later war they were "fifth columnists," quietly spreading rumors of the greatness of the khan's armies, how no one could stand against the khan; spreading fear and discontent amongst the people of Khwarezm.

Such movements have been a problem throughout

history. Merchants who filed reports, "diplomats" who sent back analysis of defenses, and tourists who had their families pose in front of bridges or defense plants before snapping a photo; all have always been the way of things, but for the great and all-powerful shah the idea that such third-class barbarians posed a danger to the kingdom while walking about it, was observed. Thus when word came that a border governor had despoiled a Mongol caravan of its goods and sent the "merchants" packing, there was no reprimand. The governor's claim that the caravan was a cover for spies was accepted. Besides, it would teach the rabble a lesson, should they indeed have other designs.

Months passed and the shah contemplated his alternatives. The Mongols were thousands of miles away, engaged in their continued raiding war in northern China. Even if they should decide to respond, a march of half a year or more would be required to bring their forces across the vast steppes of southern Siberia. The land could not support such numbers, and once at the border of Khwarezm they would be met by a host of half a million men. The fly could then be swatted, and the power and prestige of the shah would be known throughout the world for ridding civilization of such a noisome pest.

Then ambassadors from the khan arrived. Their language was not quite that of the refined and cultured ambassadors of the world of Islam but the message was clear enough. Genghis was not amused. In good faith he had allowed merchants of Khwarezm to venture into his realms, and now his own children had been robbed by a government official in the land of the shah. Full restitution plus damages must be paid at once and the offending governor punished.

It was the moment for a lesson and Shah Muhammad had a wonderful idea on how to deliver it. All of the Mongols were seized by soldiers of the guard, dragged to an open brazier and, to the vast amusement of the shah and his court, the beards of the Mongols were burned off. It must have been a rather strange sight (and smelled awful as well) as flames consumed the flowing whiskers of the ambassador and his retinue. According to some sources the ambassador was given the extra treatment of a shave that cut so close it removed his head from his body.

One will always wonder what motivated the shah at this moment. Were his own "spies" so overconfident that their reports on the Mongols were dismissive, declaring them to be nothing but ill-smelling barbarians who could be stopped by any modern army? Did he want to provoke a war he thought he could win? Throughout history there have been ways of declaring war outside of formal declarations, and such a tactic as the shah's war certainly is insulting and treacherous enough to enrage the khan. Or was he simply concerned about courtly amusement? His lesson brought howls of laughter from the court as the barbarians screamed in pain and humiliation, and then were unceremoniously kicked out the door. For weeks afterwards the court must have buzzed with just how witty the shah was to come up with such a good idea for a response.

And then the storm hit. One does not burn the beards of Mongol ambassadors and expect to survive. According to the ancient formula of the Mongols, war was declared with the statement that ultimately one side or the other would die, and only the Everlasting Sky knew who that would be.

With an army of little more than a hundred thousand men, Genghis Khan slashed his way into the heart of the Khwarezm Empire in 1219. Within a matter of months the bulk of the shah's army had not just been defeated, but annihilated. The following year the great city of Samarkand fell, its population put to the sword. The shah was now informed that the Mongols had instituted "the hunt," the assignment of two tumens of elite warriors to one task and one task only, to place the head of Muhammad Shah at the feet of Genghis Khan.

In panic the shah fled, pursued by the twenty thousand, who were led by the great Mongol general Subotai. The pursuit lasted for nearly two thousand miles, zigzagging across the length and breadth of his crumbling empire. Cornered at last on the shores of the Caspian Sea, he fled in a fishing boat to an island where he supposedly died of fright, his hair and beard having gone white with terror. As for his kingdom, some historians now argue that the collapse of the Khwarezm Empire was, in terms of relative losses, the most costly war in history. Upwards of 75% of the entire population was annihilated. Every city was flattened. In one case the course of a river was reversed forever when the Mongols dammed it to flood out a stronghold. And the intellectual heart of Islam was destroyed.

The campaign of Genghis stormed down to the shores of the Indian Ocean in pursuit of the remnants of the shah's broken armies. Subotai received permission to engage in a reconnaissance into unknown lands to the west and north. This drive would take him thousands of miles across the Caucasus and down into the fertile black-earth steppes of Rus, reaching to the Dnieper River before finally being recalled in 1223. The stage was set, however, for an effort fifteen years later; the invasion of Kievan Rus and Eastern Europe.

For destroying a few beards, the shah was repaid with the destruction of a continent.

Dangerous Delusion

Prester John and the Last Crusade
13th Century Europe

By Bill Fawcett

It all began in the fifth century A.D., when Nestorius, the patriarch of Constantinople, capital of the Byzantine Empire, began to preach that Jesus was merely a normal human who had been infused with the Holy Spirit, and therefore the Virgin Mary, Mother of God, wasn't really either one. Since the patriarch was the head of the Eastern Christian church, he was able to get his message out very quickly and to a large part of the Eastern Empire. This did not go over well, to put it mildly, with the rest of the church's patriarchs or with the reigning emperor. In a matter of weeks Nestorius was deposed and sent packing.

Undeterred, Nestorius continued to preach his "heresy" until he had gathered a fair number of followers. Because of his stubbornness, the former patriarch and those who would not renounce his teachings were exiled. At this time, exile meant traveling east beyond Byzantium's far-reaching sphere of influence. The Nestorians finally found a haven in India, where it was known that they continued to preach their heresy, but only to non-Christians as they were effectively the first Christians in that sprawling subcontinent. For a time the Nestorians' activities attracted some attention, but then, as the Byzantine Empire shrank, all contact was lost. All that remained was the knowledge that somewhere to the east were the descendants of the followers of Nestorius.

By the end of the twelfth century Europe was a very different place. The giant empires had splintered and shattered, and from Kiev to London kingdoms were small, rarely well financed, and generally unconcerned with anything beyond their borders, except maybe with freeing Jerusalem and the rest of the "Holy Land." This was probably just as well since virtually all trade beyond Europe had been cut off by the rise of Islam. This was also the end of the "Dark Ages," which had fostered ignorance of the lands beyond Europe. Where silks that came in from China through Egypt had been plentiful in Rome a thousand years earlier, now a silk robe was rare enough to mark its wearer as nobility, if not royalty, and even a small silk gown cost five years of a yeoman's wages. The eastern two-thirds of Eurasia had returned to being an unknown, yet to be explored by Marco Polo.

In the thirteenth century the face of Europe may have been far different from that of the fifth century, but the Eastern world had changed beyond all recognition. Islam had arisen, and four Crusades had temporarily freed the Holy Land. More important than the militant Islamic caliphates was the Mongol Empire, which had already conquered China and was now looking west. Small kingdoms were the rule, and feudalism supported only small armies led by those of noble blood whose only effective force was the badly disciplined heavy cavalry of armored knights. Four great Crusades had opened the Near East to trade, but bankrupted much of Christendom in the effort. The Catholic church still reigned supreme, and the pope remained the most important political figure in Europe. Much of his control derived from the Crusades he could call in the effort to free "the Holy Land" from the Moslem "infidels."

But the memory of Nestorius and his followers had evolved into the myth of Prester John. In 1122 an Indian priest arrived in Rome, claiming to be an envoy from a "multitude" of Nestorian Christians in India and China. In reality it appears no more than a few thousand Nestorians were practicing their version of Christianity in India, and there is no record of there being any at all in China. Still, this is what the pope wanted to hear. While rumors and even detailed reports of the growth of the Mongol Empire were passed on by Christian rulers in Eastern Europe, the distraction and support of Prester John and his army justified the calling of a new Crusade, later kown as the Fifth Crusade. After all, Prester John sounded like a powerful military leader and devoted Christian. He controlled the most powerful kingdom in the world, somewhere on the far side of the Islamic states. In 1145 the bishop of Syria sent the pope a letter saying he had reports of a Christian kingdom in the east that was sending an army to assist in retaking all of the Holy Land. By 1221, when the Crusade was called, it was taken as fact that Prester John was moving to save his fellow Christians from the Islamic armies that held sway from Spain to Persia. Even tales of the Mongol conquests were either ignored or taken as actually being the actions of Prester

John, and proof of his existence. To Western Europe, Prester John was real and the Mongols a myth.

So the pope called his Crusade. Thousands of knights died enroute to Palestine or on its battlefields. In the end Christianity lost the Holy Land entirely. But all felt at the time that it didn't matter, because Prester John would soon appear and turn the tide of the war. Furthermore he would come from the east, and they would smash the infidels between them. The power of this myth, cherished as only a last and foolish hope can be, directed the strategy of Europe for almost half a century. By the time it was refuted, the decisions the pope had made based upon it were history, as were the eventual results. Prester John didn't appear as expected, but the Mongols did. Western Europe was split by the strain of the Crusade and its failure.

Two of the largest, richest, and arguably most civilized of the Christian kingdoms were Poland and Hungary. Had they been left to develop untouched, as was the then-divided France, the "Dark Ages" might have ended a century earlier. But when the Mongols did finally begin their drive into Europe, the military establishments of the West were in disarray. This meant that when Béla IV of Hungary called on all of Christianity to defend itself (and his kingdom), no great army arose. Knights answered the call from all of Europe, but not as many as expected, and not a single Frankish or other Western king gathered his army in support. The tens of thousands who had, a few decades earlier, fought in Palestine were all dead or could not afford another war in a distant land. Poland, and then Hungary, were crushed. If the khan had not died and the Mongol armies withdrawn of their own accord, nothing remained to stop them from dominating all of Europe as far as Dublin.

Prester John was a myth. An appealing idea no more absurd than our own belief that we can have peace through Mutually Assured Destruction. Yet the idea of joining forces with a nonexistent Christian kingdom of the east after a century of defeats at the hands of Islamic armies seemed to be such a good idea that the pope, and thousands of nobles, could not resist it. A myth that, except for the khah's fortuitous demise, would have meant the Mongol conquest of all of Europe.

CRACKDOWN CRACK UP

Sicilian Vespers Massacre
1282 Palermo, Sicily

by Bill Fawcett

Since the Romans invaded, and probably before, the Sicilian people have resented being the doormat for whatever Mediterranean power is currently ascendent. This was the case in 1282, when the French monarchy controlled Sicily. In 1266, Charles of Anjou had been crowned king of Sicily. It is likely that he saw the island as a desolate place that served no real purpose beyond being a naval base and paying taxes. It is certain that the Sicilians resented his coronation, which was negotiated by major European powers without any concern for their desires or needs.

Now, in this age of rampant nationalism, it is easy to think that the Sicilians were aroused by national feelings. While there was a good deal more unity and identity in Sicily than in most of Europe at the time, this was only a small part of the problem. The most annoying aspect to Sicilians was the French monarchy's need for money, and they saw distant locations such as Sicily as good places to squeeze for every penny that could be raised. Also annoying was that French bureaucrats were brought in to collect the taxes and maintain order. These Frenchmen, likely Parisians, saw the Sicilians as unwashed provincials, which they were. The problem was, they *treated* them like unwashed provincials.

Even so, for the island that created La Cosa Nostra as a way to defend its people against occupiers, things were relatively calm. There were many little incidents and a lot of rabble rousing, but nothing major, until March 30, 1282 the Monday after Easter, when the worm turned. A crowd had gathered for the vespers service. The day before, the Sicilians had been upset that a group of French soldiers had broken into the main church for Palermo, the church of Santo Spirito (Holy Spirit), and grabbed a number of tax evaders. Doubtless this was seen to be an object lesson for the others attending that mass, if still a violation of the age-old tradition of sanctuary. The sight of men being shackled as they sat in pews aroused murmurs, but no resistance. And now, on this Monday before the mass started, hundreds of local Catholics had gathered in front of the church.

The local authorities, likely more than one, became nervous at such a large gathering. It was decided to send about 200 Frenchmen to make sure that this was only a religious festival and that all of the Sicilians were unarmed. This made perfect sense. Similar gatherings had featured rabble-rousers, and the actions of the day before, in the same place, invited problems. So troops were sent both to intimidate and to investigate the hundreds that had gathered. Resentfully, the unarmed Sicilians allowed themselves to be searched for weapons. There were none. But the French disdain was obvious and it took only a little spark to light a fire under the Sicilian's pride. One of the Frenchmen pushed his hand under a newly married woman's blouse, searching for "weapons." Her new husband was outraged. Yelling "Death to the French," he grabbed the Frenchman's sword from its scabbard and ran him through. This set off the crowd. Without arms of their own, they nonetheless managed to kill virtually all of the French soldiers, while records indicate the Sicilians suffered two hundred casualties of their own.

In the next days the population rioted. Thousands of Frenchmen were killed and anyone who married or collaborated with them also died.

Charles reacted by sending more troops, who retook Sicily and viciously oppressed the Sicilians. Revolt and resistance became a way of life. The people grew to have allegiance to their own shadow governments, establishing a cultural pattern that led to the infamous Cosa Nostra as we know it today. So the rather routine, if unnecessary and rude, crowd policing not only gave rise to a rebellion, but created the very mechanism that gave rise to the first organized crime in America. You have to wonder how many bodies in trunks, or wearing cement overshoes, can be laid at the feet of that obscure thirteenth century bureaucrat's decision to make sure there was no trouble at a religious festival.

A PLAGUE ON ALL YOUR MOUSES

A Black Day for Cats
Europe 1300s

by Jody Lynn Nye

The plague that came to be known as the Black Death first appeared in China during the early 1300s. Victims reported feeling achy, feverish, and nauseated. Purple lumps appeared in the armpit and groin area that quickly swelled to the size of hen's eggs and hardened. If the lumps burst, stinking, black matter gushed forth, but relief was usually too late for the victim, who died within three to five days of onset. No cure was known, and no preventive measure seemed to be effective. Within eighty years the illness reduced the Chinese population by a third. By infecting host after host along the well-traveled trade routes, the plague spread westward toward India and the Middle East, killing thousands of people per day.

The vector of infection at the time was unknown. In 1347, steppe warriors infected a besieged Genoese town in the Crimea by throwing dead bodies into its midst with a catapult. Most of the town contracted the disease. The bodies of the dead were collected and burned so the germs would not spread to the living, but the plague continued unabated. Escaping from their ruined city, the Genoese sailed home to Sicily and introduced the plague into a new and wholly unsuspecting population. From there, the epidemic spread throughout Europe and north Africa, killing millions.

The name Black Death came to be applied to the plague because of the dark purple color the sufferer's skin turned in the last stages of the disease. The coloration was due to the reduction of oxygen in the blood, a sign of respiratory failure. No medical technique of the day could stop the disease once it took hold. While it is only fatal in approximately three in four cases, that was enough to wipe out whole towns and whip European civilization into a panic.

Doctors searched for a way to stop the plague. Patients were quarantined within their houses, but the disease still spread like a forest fire. Many people thought the Black Death had been visited upon them because God was angry with them for living sinful lives. In order to placate God, people sought out scapegoats. Some pilgrims beat themselves, hoping to draw divine wrath upon them and not on their fellow man. Others, notably in Brussels and Strasbourg, blamed the presence of Jews for the epidemic. Thousands were murdered in the ensuing panic. Others claimed the Black Death was caused by witchcraft. Harmless men and women were carried from their homes and hanged or burned in an effort to stop the progress of the disease. Cats, because of their glowing eyes and habit of going abroad by night, were popularly felt to be magical familiars of these witches. They were slaughtered in the thousands. By killing the cats, however, the Europeans were destroying one of their first lines of defense against the plague.

Bubonic plague, or *Yersinia pestis*, is carried by the common rat flea. Rats were everywhere during the Middle Ages. Sanitation was primitive. The streets were open sewers through which human waste, garbage, and the remains of dead animals sluggishly flowed. Black plague spread by the proliferation of germ-carrying fleas, which lived on the backs of rats. The ship that carried the Genoese back to Europe was infested with infected rats that came ashore with the humans, bringing their fleas with them. If the hordes of cats that usually frequented the waterfront had been allowed to live, they would have killed the rats. Instead, the rodents bred unchecked, carrying their fleas into millions of now unprotected households.

The plague returned five times more to Europe during the fourteenth century. By its end over a third of the population was dead. If the cats had been left alone, the mortality rate among humans would have been greatly lessened.

NEVER LOOK A GIFT CANNON IN THE MOUTH

A Very Urban Attitude
1453 Constantinople

by William R. Forstchen

When facing a war one should not only consider the state of one's own technology, but also what new technologies one's opponent might bring to bear.

For over seven hundred years the great city of Constantinople had faced repeated assaults from the Islamic world, first from the initial out-sweep of Arab conquerors in the seventh through ninth centuries, and later from the Ottoman Turks, who came into the region in the twelfth century. It was high technology which had saved the city through the introduction of Greek Fire, a mixture of naphtha and pitch. The napalm of its day, the secret brew was loaded aboard ships, and through an ingenious system of bellows fired from a bronze cannon. With a range of over fifty yards, no wooden ship could stand against it. Similar flamethrowers were mounted along the massive walls of the city and thus, for seven hundred years, the city sur-

vived repeated assaults, even while the rest of its empire
was inexorably chipped away.

By the early fifteenth century the only piece of the
once mighty empire that still survived was the city itself
and a few small islands in the Aegean. In 1451 Mohammed II, "the Conqueror," came to the Ottoman throne
and vowed that the goal of seven hundred years would
be achieved—the mighty city of Constantinople would fall
to the sword of Islam. Marshaling his armies, he sent out
notices that any and all who came to him with a means
of breaching the city, whether they were Christian, Moslem or Jew, would be well rewarded.

The new art of cannon making had only been around
for a couple of generations. The weapons were small,
crude, and highly inaccurate, with ranges not much beyond a hundred yards. The powder was volatile and dangerous, and its ingredients, charcoal, saltpeter and sulfur,
tended to separate during shipment and storage (the secret of soaking the powder after mixing it, then drying
and grinding it, had yet to be developed).

Though this new weapon system showed some promise it was still seen as little more than a very noisy toy,
in the same way that the first Wright Flyers were little
more than dangerous kites and yet were harbingers of the
Messerschmitts and Spitfires to come.

Urban of Hungary had a fascination with cannons,
and he seized upon a rather dramatic solution for the
weak powder and inaccuracy that then prevailed. If one
was simply to increase the scale of the weapon, to make
it humongous, a veritable leviathan, accuracy and power
would no longer matter. The sheer size of the ball would
make it deadly once you got it into the air. His dream
weapon was a true monster, a cannon with a forty-eight-

inch bore firing a stone ball weighing more than a ton. Backing up this supercannon would be several guns firing thirty-six-inch shot, down to lighter weapons loaded with hundreds of small stones, designed to protect the superweapons and sweep away any sorties that might venture out of a besieged city.

Needless to say the weapons would be slightly expensive. The supergun would require one of the largest castings ever, and hundreds of dangerous wagonloads of powder would be needed to support it.

Urban knew he had a winner with this weapon system and, like any good arms merchant, he started to shop the idea around. The obvious candidate for a contract was Constantinople. The armies of Mohammed II were gathering on the eastern shore of the Dardanelles, and the leader of the Turks was openly proclaiming a holy war against the city.

Undoubtedly there was at least a tiny bit of religious and racial identity on the part of Urban when he approached the advisors to Emperor Constantine XI. He set forth his plan, pointing out that any city armed with these new superweapons would be invulnerable to attack. One blast from the mighty bombard could sweep down hundreds of attackers or sink a ship. If the enemy dared to array similar weapons they could be torn apart before inflicting any damage, and as for siege towers, they'd be blown to splinters.

He was rejected. The advisors decided the cost of the untested bombards would be far better spent on hiring additional mercenaries. It seems no one seriously considered that Urban's second stop would be right across the straits, for he was, after all, an arms dealer. Mohammed

II immediately seized on the new weapons and contracted Urban to provide them.

A year later Mohammed's army laid siege to the city, and Urban's mighty bombards were the deciding factor. The weapons were placed well beyond the range of the Greek flamethrowers, and protected from the archery of the mercenaries hired with the money that might have been spent on the guns instead.

The walls were breached, the Turks swarmed in, and Constantine XI died gallantly trying to stop the breakthrough. One would like to think that the advisors who vetoed Urban died at his side but such justice rarely happens.

As to Urban's good idea of selling his weapon to the Turks, that might have been the worst thing of all in the long run. With Constantinople no longer a barrier of defense but rather the new capital of the Ottoman Empire, all of southeastern Europe became a battlefield. Twice the Turkish waves reached all the way to Vienna, and Urban's homeland became a scorched battlefield. His desire to make a killing on his idea helped unleash over five hundred years of strife in the region, strife which bedevils Hungary even today.

ONE DISPENSATION TOO MANY

Pope Refuses to Grant Henry VIII a Second Dispensation
1533 Rome and England

By Brian Thomsen

Papal dispensations, by their very nature as the means to undo or excuse the act of an individual(s) whose behavior violates one of God's laws, must be few and far between.

Of course, not even the Catholic Church has managed to hold itself to the highest standards, and in an era not too far removed from the age when numerous popes had mistresses and children, such papal dispensations could usually be obtained quite quietly for a substantial donation to the Vatican treasury.

Thus, in 1503, when Ferdinand of Spain petitioned the pontiff, Julius II, for a dispensation that would allow his daughter Katherine to marry the eleven-year-old Prince Henry of England, a Bull of Dispensation was expected to be granted. Though Katherine had indeed been married to Henry's older brother, who was alleged to have died prior to physically consummating their union, the pope did not hesitate to point out that Leviticus strictly forbade a man to marry his brother's wife and warned that such unions would be cursed with childlessness. However an alliance and an extremely large dowry (a portion of which would wind up in papal coffers) were at stake, and, as a result, the dispensation was granted. In two years Henry Tudor, future king of England, was to be married to Katherine of Aragon—five and a half years his senior.

Spain, England, and Rome all looked on the union and smiled as they counted their financial rewards; even though the actual wedding did not take place until June 11, 1509, four years later than originally planned. Henry had ascended to the throne of England as King Henry VIII two months earlier and things looked rosy for the young royal couple.

Henry was by all accounts a good king, an artist, an athlete, and a scholar. He was lusty and full of life, and more than ready to sire a long line of kings to follow him. Katherine deeply desired to assist him in this pursuit, even adopting the pomegranate, the symbol of fertility, as her personal badge. Unfortunately, by 1518 she had been pregnant no less than six times, bearing three boys and three girls, with only one of the six, a daughter, Mary, surviving infancy.

Henry was by no means thrilled, having been denied a son to follow him, as well as having to be married to a woman five years his senior who was more than beginning to show the wear and tear of six pregnancies. She had lost her looks, and had become deeply religious. Young and lusty Henry had no choice but to turn an eye elsewhere in search of a younger woman who might bear him the prince he owed his people.

Henry's attention soon turned toward a certain young woman of the court by the name of Anne Boleyn, who he described as "a young lady who has the soul of an angel and a spirit worthy of a crown." Ambitious to a fault, Anne had no desire to become just another one of the king's mistresses. Anne wanted to be queen, and Henry wanted male heirs to the throne. It seemed like a match made in heaven. There was just one catch—Henry was still married to Katherine, and she had no desire to let him go.

No problem, thought the king.

Cardinal Wolsey, one of the king's advisors, immediately petitioned the new pope, Clement, for a new dispensation that would annul Henry's marriage to Katherine on the grounds that the first dispensation had been ill-advised. Such a dispensation would also remove Katherine's daughter, Mary, from the line of succession as she would be made retroactively the product of a union outside of wedlock and thus illegitimate.

Agents of Katherine and her family had already contacted the Vatican to plead their case, explaining that the king only wanted the divorce for private reasons, and was obsessed with a woman far from worthy of him. Wolsey countered by citing the need for a male heir to the throne, Anne Boleyn's virtues, and alleged diseases that kept the current queen from ever again fulfilling her wifely duties to the king.

Negotiations dragged out, were further complicated by the political, financial, and social ripples the annulment would cause throughout Europe; as well as by Anne's alleged Reformist beliefs. The latter were quickly communicated to Rome via the Spanish ambassadors, whose nationalist interests obviously sided with Katherine.

Henry soon became impatient with Rome, whose sympathy toward Spain was not the least of England's

problems. The real problem lay with Clement's own reluctance to undo the "divinely inspired work" of one of his
predecessors.

At Anne's urging, and driven by his own lust and
desire for an heir, Henry finally broke off all negotiations
with Rome, and established the reformed Church of England. He quickly appointed himself the head, married
Anne, and had his first marriage annulled.

Henry was excommunicated, but didn't mind as he
now had his own church that he could bend to his will.

The Church of England has lasted far longer than his
marriage to Anne did. It is still thriving—whereas Anne
was divorced via execution on Friday, May 19, 1536, a
little less than three and a half years after her wedding
to Henry. She left behind a daughter and no male heirs.
But it seemed like a good idea to the ruler the pope had
only a few year earlier give the title "Defender of the
Faith."

WRONG TURN

An Intact Armada Turns North
1588 Spanish Armada

by Bill Fawcett

There were a number of perfectly valid reason why his "most Catholic majesty," King Philip II of Spain decided to assemble an armada and invade England. England was a Protestant country and the devout Philip had been declared "Defender of the Faith" by the pope. Politically, England was a growing power that was challenging the long-dominant Spain for colonies and trade. England had recently meddled heavily in Spain's attempt to put down a series of revolts in the Spanish Netherlands. And the English privateers, particularly Sir Frances Drake, had become a serious annoyance. Drake had not only pillaged and sacked a major Spanish colony in Panama, but he and his cohorts had captured a number of treasure ships— ships of the Gold and Plate fleets, which financed most of the Spanish government's budget.

The invasion plan was simple. Philip had the Duke of Medina-Sidonia gather and construct an armada con-

sisting of about forty warships—towering, massive galleons armed with dozens of short ranged, but very
powerful cannons—and an even greater number of transport and supply vessels. The fleet was complemented by
nineteen thousand soldiers.

This great force would then join up with an even
larger army of veteran troops under the command of the
Duke of Parma, who commanded the Spanish armies in
the Spanish Netherlands. The sole purpose of the armada
was to load this army on board and land it on the English
coast. Should they accomplish this, it was almost inevitable that England could be conquered.

The Spanish infantry was undisputedly the best
trained and most effective in Europe. Their musket and
pike formations had defeated all opposition for over a
century. Only the Swiss schiltrons could match them, and
luckily for Spain England wasn't their ally. Once the infantry made it ashore, it seemed likely that the small English army and the poorly trained militia would be
crushed. This meant that, to survive, England had to deal
with the threat while it was still at sea, in the English
Channel.

To meet the armada in battle the English assembled
an even larger fleet, one of more than one hundred and
sixty warships, in her southern ports; however, these
ships were much different from Spain's. Smaller and with
thinner hulls, the British ships were designed for speed
and maneuverability rather than staying power and
weight of shot. The guns on the English ships were different as well. These cannon were longer barreled and of a
much smaller caliber than those on the Spanish galleons.
Their greater length meant they could throw a cannon

ball much farther, but these balls were often half the size of those used in the much shorter-ranged Spanish guns.

Thus, while the English could fire and hit the enemy ships from outside the range of the armada's guns, the balls that hit would rarely do any real damage when combined with the thick hulls of the Spanish ships, many simply bouncing off galleons' thick wood. But if the smaller English ships closed to where their guns could do some real damage they would find themselves within range of the heavier Spanish guns. Their larger balls would wreak havoc on any English ship. So a straight fire fight in the cause of defending England was out of the question.

Boarding the Spanish ships as they traveled up the Channel was also not an option. The Spanish Armada kept a tight formation, so any English ship close enough to board any Spanish warship would be annihilated by others nearby. And although the English kept the Spanish under hours of near constant, but basically ineffective, long-range fire by the English commanded by Charles Howard and led into combat by long time enemy Sir Frances Drake, the armada maintained its planned formation with little difficulty. There was also the minor matter of size. The Spanish ships towered over the smaller English vessels, had much larger crews, and were ferrying the nineteen thousand battle-ready soldiers.

So the English were unable to prevent the Spanish Armada from sailing toward the Netherlands and Parma's army. Spain suffered minimal losses and few worries, for they had no need to actually defeat the English navy. Simply landing Parma's army in England would guarantee a Spanish victory. So things were looking good and the Duke of Medina-Sidonia had confidence in the plan's success until the armada reached the Netherlands and discovered Parma's troops weren't ready to embark. The timing was off and it would be several days before the thousands of men he commanded could all board their waiting ships.

Thus the Spanish Armada, fearing approaching rough weather, placed itself near the coast by the port of Calais. In a tight formation capable of driving off any English ships that might venture too close, the armada waited. This gave the English a chance to deal with them using a classic weapon of that era, fire ships.

On the day after the armada anchored, August 7, 1588, eight fireships were sailed into the anchored Spanish ships. Now a fire ship wasn't just an ordinary ship that had been set on fire. Though the wooden ships and canvas sails burned amazingly well, and fire was always a concern on any ship during the age of sail, fire ships such as the English used were smeared from stem to stern with pitch, tar, and other flammable substances. Barrels of the same were then broken open on the deck to ensure no one was going to extinguish their flames once the fire was lit. Then, just to make sure that no one tried to simply tow the burning ships away, some fire ships were also packed with gunpowder. Sailors were understandably reluctant to cast a line on and stay near a fire ship when it might blow them both out of the water, literally, at any time.

To attack with a fire ship, the understandably limited complement of sailors on board lines up the ship and fixes the rudder so the wind will push it toward the target. The crewmen then torch the fire ship and abandon it for smaller boats. While the wind sometimes blew fire ships astray, on this occasion providence favored the English.

When the eight fire ships descended on the tightly packed armada, panic ensued. Though only a few ships of the Spanish fleet were actually damaged by the fires themselves, the disciplined formation that had held the English seamen at bay was lost. Ships scattered wildly into the Channel, enabling two or three English warships to close with an isolated Spanish ship and overwhelm it. A confused melee followed where the English ships, built for speed and maneuverability, had a huge advantage. By nightfall over a dozen of the great warships had been destroyed or captured, and the ships of the Spanish Armada were spread for miles.

More than one hundred Spanish ships still remained, however. And although they were short of powder and shot, they were still a force equal to the English, who, unknown to the Spanish, had completely depleted their supply of powder and shot. When the English were forced to pull back as a result, the remnants of the armada were able to regroup.

Now comes the decision which puts this bit of history in this book. The Duke of Medina-Sidonia was not a sailor, but he was faced with an untenable naval situation. Most of his armada was intact, but limited their ability to meet the English again by their lack of powder and shot. They had been forced out of the only large port in the area and the weather was turning rough; the English Channel with its rocky shores was no place to try to ride out a storm. Also, there was no further hope of landing the Duke of Parma's army anywhere. So clearly, the wisest thing to do would be to sail for Spain. They could build more ships over the winter and try again in the spring. Unfortunately, the English fleet was still waiting below the Spanish in the Channel. They too had suffered

few losses, and the Duke did not know they had expended all their ammunition. So he decided his best
course was to avoid another confrontation by taking the
"safe" way home; they would turn north and sail around
England and Ireland.

The decision created several complications. The ships
were all packed with sailors and soldiers. Most quickly
ran short of food. The waters were unfamiliar to the Spanish captains, who were forced to stay far offshore for fear
of unknown shoals. The wild and gray North Sea was no
place for tall Spanish galleons designed for much calmer
Mediterranean waters. And even in August, the air over
the North Sea is rarely warm and the water always freez-
ing cold. Men accustomed to the mild weather of Iberia
actually froze to death trying to sail the ships. These problems were aggravated by two weeks of storms which accomplished what the English navy could not. Well over
half the ships of the Spanish Armada were forced onto
the rocky Scottish and Irish coasts. Even when the ships
managed to survive the ordeal, many of the crewmen
were washed overboard or died of exposure. Bodies
washed ashore by the hundreds.

When the remnants of the armada returned to Spain,
it was not immediately apparent that their defeat was the
beginning of the end for Spain as the dominant power in
Europe. But England could now confidently take a more
aggressive and independent stand on any issue, knowing
that her ships could protect the island nation from retribu-
tion, while Philip II squandered a great deal of wealth
stolen from the Americas in constructing a second armada, before scrapping the idea. Two hundred years later
the sun couldn't set on the British Empire while Spain

had been reduced to a backward, minor player in European politics.

Had the armada sailed south and confronted the English and their empty powder chests, there would have been little the English could have done and the threat of invasion would have remained. But it seemed like a good idea to the Spanish duke that they sail north, and history was changed forever.

HOW TO LOSE AN EMPIRE

Mercenaries and the American Revolution
1776 America

by William R. Forstchen

Few had originally intended it to be an outright revolution. The encounter at Lexington Green was, first and foremost, an accident. The ninety-odd militia men had gathered on the green with the intent of *protesting* the advance of a British column out of Boston. Great events usually only become great in retrospect, and the early days of the revolution only became truly revolutionary after the show was over.

Few really wanted a war, and when both sides backed into one there was outright confusion on the part of the colonials as to what they were truly fighting for during the first months. There were a few people, like Sam Adams, who were screaming for independence, but most ordinary citizens looked upon him as a wild-eyed radical. Moderates, including the likes of Ben Franklin, looked back on their history as *Englishmen* and saw things differently. Only ninety years in the past a bloodless coup, the

Glorious Revolution of 1688, had affirmed the rights of all Englishmen and clearly resolved the fact that government existed solely through the consent of the governed. Many believed, with some justification, that a significant number of representatives in Parliament were actually in support of the colonial cause, seeing the fight there as a continuance of the struggle for political freedom against the crown that had gone on during the previous century.

Thus, when the Continental Congress dispatched Washington to organize a Continental Army to besiege the British troops in Boston, it also dispatched letters of grievance to England. In short, the vast majority wanted nothing more than to go back to being Englishmen.

Voices were raised in Parliament in support of the colonials. Some even ventured to offer that, if the issue was truly over taxation without representation, there was nothing wrong with providing extra seats in Parliament and thereby defusing the crisis. But the thousand casualties from Breed's Hill were hard to ignore. The incredible stupidity of the British commander who had ordered a frontal assault against a heavily fortified position was brushed over by the conservatives. More than one son of good gentleman's blood had died in that assault, and to brush it under the rug was unthinkable.

In the center of this was the king. Now, two-hundred-odd years of American history has painted this man into a bloody corner. For after all, when one fights a war for independence that costs the lives of tens of thousands, someone has to be the fall guy, and George III is it. In actuality he wasn't all that bad a character. Granted, he did have his faults, such as going insane due to a bio-chemical imbalance, but that was later. Like most of the Hanoverian kings of the eighteenth century, he wasn't really noted as a great intellect. The gene pool for George's family seems to have been a bit shallow when it came to brains, but he was dedicated to just doing his job, being a promoter of the sciences and arts, and, unlike many of his contemporaries, he was a loving family man.

When presented with the losses from the fighting around Boston he was shocked, saddened, and outraged. George was something of a detail man, the type who could take a report and stare at it for hours; and the only way he had of getting any information about the situation in the colonies was through reading reports from royal governors, government administrators, and military officers. Perhaps that should have been warning enough to him right there, given the corrupt English practice of selling such offices to the highest bidder. A few have even suggested that if he had taken the unprecedented step of sending a committee of royal representatives to the Americas to investigate the situation, or better yet, gone himself, or at least agreed to a meeting with a delegation from the Continental Congress, the entire crisis would have fizzled away.

There was another game lingering beneath the surface however. George's family line was not actually British. Through a complicated and somewhat bizarre decision-making process back at the turn of the century, the English had found themselves without a monarch after the deaths of William and Mary (Dutch nobility brought in to rule after the revolution of 1688). Not trusting any of their own royal blood, the English had invited the royal line of the German state of Hanover to come and take up the office when no one could agree on anyone else. George's grandfather, the first British ruler of that name, couldn't even speak English. Thus, for most of the eighteenth century, Germans had sat on the throne, and had sensed the slightly veiled scorn of the upper crust, which viewed them as uncouth upstarts. Over in France Louis XVI ran his show without question; Frederick of Prussia would have laughed himself sick at the mere suggestion of dealing with armed and rebellious peasants, then ordered the army out to shoot them all; and Catherine of Russia was constantly bedeviled by such rebellions, and usually knocked off a few tens of thousands in response. Even the cultured Hapsburgs of Austria never would have dreamed of having to argue with a parliament over money, or contemplated sitting down at the table with the leaders of a rebellion to talk things out over a cup of tea.

Thus began to form what, from the perspective of poor George, must have seemed like a good idea. These were royal colonies with royal charters and appointed governors. Weakness was the one thing a king, especially a king who had a throne based on an uncomfortable compromise worked out years earlier, could not show. He could never let it be said that while he was king the richest colonies in the world had been lost. Nor could he appear to show weakness by dealing with traitors in open rebellion against his rightful authority. Thus it came down to who would have to make the first move toward reconciliation, and George, thinking like a king, expected it to be the colonists who did it first.

The initial overtures by the Continental Congress to negotiate a way out of the rebellion fell entirely on deaf ears. Franklin and the other delegates never even got past the front door of the palace (and it should be remembered that Ben was something of an international celebrity in 1775; an honored scientist, author, and social commentator). The word that came down from Windsor was that there would be no negotiations while an armed mob sat outside Boston. The rabble had to disband and go home, rightful British authority had to be reasserted, and only then would grievances be listened to. One can almost picture George's aides nodding their heads with approval, muttering that this would show the world, and Parliament, who had backbone and who didn't.

This particular idea came up short. The fight along Concord Road, and especially the debacle at Breed's Hill, had radicalized the situation. More than one colonial leader suspected that if they ever disarmed, vengeful squads of British soldiers would be at their doorsteps. With negotiations out, the process started to roll forward. What had begun as a containment of British forces inside Boston now shifted to an open siege. Washington sent a rotund bookseller, Henry Knox, who claimed to have read up on artillery, off to Fort Ticondaroga to lift out the heavy weapons and drag them clear across Massachusetts in the dead of winter to give the colonials the firepower to knock the British out of town.

George, who had actually believed that his hard-line stance in the beginning would have the desired effect, was shocked. He never expected to need his army and the colonists' response put him in a bad spot. Ever since the Civil War the English on both sides had a healthy fear of a standing military. Regiments were needed but, except for a very small force at home, the majority were committed overseas . . . where they would never pose a political threat. When the colonists refused to back down, George's military advisors told him that it would take at least fifty thousand men to stop the rebellion . . . in itself a typically arrogant military forecast. This would require mobilizing at least fifteen to twenty additional regiments in England. Such an action would require significant cooperation from a Parliament already divided on how to handle this crisis, and the heavy recruitment of tens of thousands of new officers and soldiers who might not be all that willing to go off to the wilds of America.

Where to get more men without taxing England? Why Germany, of course; he had a lot of contacts with cousins all over Germany. This was long prior to the unification of Germany and, except for Prussia and Bavaria, most of the region was divided into dozens of small kingdoms, whose national pride demanded that they have some kind of army of at least a few regiments. Following the model of Frederick of Prussia, the armies of these small states were precise, well drilled, and highly disciplined units, but terribly expensive for such small states to maintain. The answer, George thought, was simple . . . rent the German armies.

A great solution. It would alleviate the need to raise new regiments in England, the troops were already highly trained, and would definitely show the colonials that he was serious. As for the German rulers, it was an excellent idea. Not only would the cost of running the units be taken care of, but there'd actually be a profit, and those who survived the expedition would return as highly trained veterans with true combat experience, something not seen since the Seven Years War a generation earlier.

So the contract was made and well over twenty thousand German troops were retained. It would take months to organize the men, outfit them for an overseas expedition (the largest transoceanic expedition in history up to that time), and put together the necessary logistical supports.

Early in the spring of 1776 word exploded across the colonies that the crown had summarily rejected any attempts at negotiation, but worst, infinitely worse, was the news that a major expeditionary force was being assembled which would contain foreign mercenaries. How dare they bring outsiders into this family squabble? Because the colonists still saw themselves as English. In fact, the majority still saw themselves as loyal Englishmen. Now the king was sending foreign troops to invade and suppress the rights of Englishmen to protest unjust laws! This one decision, perhaps more than any other instituted between June 1775 and July 1776, served to push the moderates who had hoped for a peaceful resolution into the ranks of the radicals, who had been calling for a full-blown revolution. In turn, it took the vast majority of Americans who had been sitting on the fence and radicalized them as well. Even some who had been open loyalists in those first months now switched sides, for who could fight for a king who would unleash foreign hordes on English soil?

The anticipated Germans landed in New York the following month, the first of well over twenty thousand; historically known as Hessians since a significant portion came from the principality of Hesse to serve in the American war. By 1778 France was on our side, and on several occasions French and German troops would square off against each other. In general the German troops fought with professionalism and maintained strict discipline when interacting with the civilian population, but their mere presence was provocation enough for the Revolutionaries. A careful read of the Declaration of Independence, where the grievances against the king are listed, will reveal a clear and direct statement denouncing the use of foreign mercenaries, Less than half of them would return to Germany; thousands dying from disease, battle, and in prisons. Thousands more, contemplating what they had to go back to, deserted, some going into the revolutionary ranks, most simply disappearing into the civilian population. Militarily they made little difference in the final outcome. Politically they might very well have served to turn George's good idea into one of the underlying causes for the birth of this nation.

FROM PAPER TO
REALITY, HOW TO LOSE A WAR

Howe and the Campaign of 1777
1777 United States

by William R. Forstchen

The first full year of campaigning against the American revolutionary armies appeared to have brought victory within easy grasp, and Lord George Germain, Secretary of State for the Colonies, knew that just one more season would end it all. He had studied the maps of the colonies and the reports from his field commander, Lord William Howe. For the moment New England was the hotbed of the rebellion, but in the middle Atlantic region, especially New York and New Jersey, support was now swinging back to a loyalist stance. During the winter of 1776, when Washington's rabble was being driven across New Jersey, not a single militiaman had turned out in support. Germain felt that if New England could be cut off from the other colonies and isolated, the rebellion would simmer down and die.

Gazing at the maps, he saw an obvious and direct approach to end the affair. General Burgoyne was operating out of the Saint Lawrence River valley in loyalist Canada. He had all but defeated the mob army during a summer campaign in upstate New York, but was forced to withdraw back into Canada due to the onset of winter. In New York City to the south, Howe, with nearly twenty thousand men, was sitting out the winter as well, while the all but defeated army of Washington froze in the woods of western New Jersey.

Germain reasoned that all that was needed was a simple linkup. Once the spring snows cleared Burgoyne should come down from the north, moving along the vast open highway provided by Lakes Champlain and George. From the south end of Lake George it was less than eighty miles to Albany, a week's leisurely march on good roads. And the same stood for Howe's army. Howe's brother was in charge of the supporting fleet accompanying the army, and the Hudson was a tidal river all the way up to Albany. A week's sail northward and the two armies would be together. To add additional punch, a small third army could come up the Mohawk from the west. Of course there'd be some resistance, but that was the whole point of the exercise. Washington would have to come out of hiding to block Howe's advance, and the annoying mob to the north under the less-than-competent St. Clair would have to try to block Burgoyne. The two mighty British armies would squeeze the resistance between them, with Howe's fleet providing support. The colonial armies in the north and middle Atlantic would die, New England would be isolated, and the show would essentially be over except for the formality of a surrender by the pitiful rebels.

Germain's plan seemed like a true winner, a grand scheme, mapped out in the drawing rooms and parlors of the colonial office and most likely presented to the king with approving advisors and courtiers nodding in agreement.

Contemporary observers who had served in the Americas, and later historians sifting through all the paperwork, have both commented that one of the greatest failings of the British colonial office's management of the war was that they were absolutely clueless as to the reality of conditions in America. Staring at a map they never quite grasped that one could take all of Great Britain, drop it into a corner of the thirteen colonies, and still have a couple of hundred thousand square miles left over. When they saw a road on a map they envisioned it as the highway between London and Portsmouth rather than the ribbon of mud which it usually was. They also forgot that colonials armed with axes often dropped thousands of trees as they retreated.

Next was the simple issue of coordination. In 1777 half a dozen separate commands were operating in the Americas . . . forces in Canada, western New York, New York City, loyalist units in the south, a fleet in New York City, and other fleets and units operating along the coasts and in the Caribbean—without a local, centralized command. Every order, every allocation of supplies, every purchase order, commendation, change of command, major troop movement, and request for reinforcements had to be routed all the way across the Atlantic to the office of Lord Germain. Even in the best of conditions it could take two months for a single request to be sent across, processed, and sent back.

So Germain blithely ordered the three-pronged assault, which would culminate with the seizure of Albany and a hoped-for pitched battle somewhere near that town that would destroy the main colonial armies, for the year 1777. And made one glaring mistake.

When all the plans were drawn up, and orders cut, somehow the phrasing of the orders to Lord Howe left him with discretionary powers as to how he would actually operate the summer campaign—without a single direct instruction. Perhaps it was because Howe was a gentleman, and one didn't give gentlemen curt, preemptive orders, or perhaps it was the failure of a clerk to copy everything down precisely. Regardless of the reasons, by the time Howe received his orders, after the courier ship had spent weeks at sea, the lord commander in New York interpreted everything to read that he had the final say over how to defeat Washington.

Meanwhile, in the north, Burgoyne had received his orders as well and doggedly started his campaign into upstate New York. Every foot of what was called a road had to be cleared of trees dropped by retreating colonials. A column sent up to Bennington to seize much-needed supplies was cut off and wiped out. By the middle of August Burgoyne was in trouble; he was too far in now to retreat all the way back to Canada. Yet at this key juncture a note finally arrived from Lord Howe . . . it was a simple "good luck Johnnie, but I'm off to Philadelphia." Lord Howe had decided to turn south.

Howe had tried to lure Washington into a fight, but with each British advance Washington would pull back toward the wilderness of western New Jersey, and Howe was in no mood to go chasing off into the forests like Burgoyne. Why couldn't Washington just play by the rules of a gentleman? Howe contemplated doing as Germain *suggested*, by taking the northern route to link up with Burgoyne, but there was no guarantee that Washing-

ton would necessarily fight. Second, there were the difficult fortifications at the narrows of the Hudson around
West Point that would have to be forced, and at the end
of it all he might very well go all the way to Albany while
Washington stayed in the New York area to seize the
main base of British operations.

The rebels had declared the city of Philadelphia to be
their capital and therefore, Howe reasoned, a campaign
to take that city would draw Washington out for a real
stand-up fight, the kind of battle that favored the experienced British troops over the less well-trained rebel army.
Howe's first impulse was to sail his entire army up the
Delaware River on his brother's fleet. The Delaware River
actually had some forts along it, so he decided to sail all
the way south to the Chesapeake, then go all the way up
the Bay and disembark at Head of Elk, modern day Elk-
ton. There were some noises made by the staff and his
brother about supporting Burgoyne but Howe shrugged
them off. Burgoyne was certainly all right, Howe reasoned.
Once his own army was dropped off, his brother could sail
back, take a couple of thousand men if need be, and venture back up the Hudson with plenty of time to spare. In
the meantime Washington would fight for Philadelphia, be
defeated, the city would surrender, Congress would surrender, and Washington himself would surrender once his
capital was lost.

So, in late July, Howe headed south with nearly his
entire force, leaving behind a garrison of seven thousand
men under Clinton and a small fleet in New York harbor.
There was only one big problem with all of this. He never
bothered to clear it with Germain first, nor did he even
advise Burgoyne of his thoughts until "Gentleman Johnnie" was already deep into the wilderness and too far

forward to retreat. Howe made his way into the Chesapeake, and Washington finally came to battle along Brandywine Creek on September 11, 1777. He was defeated as expected, but did not surrender.

Two days after Brandywine, two hundred miles to the north, Burgoyne made the desperate move of crossing the Hudson River at Saratoga, New York, with the intent of racing on to Albany, where he hoped to find enough supplies and shelter to survive the approaching winter. He ran directly into the colonial army, entrenched and blockading the road, while additional colonial troops started to circle around his flanks and rear, cutting off his supply line to Canada. There was only one hope left, that his desperate pleas for help, smuggled through the colonial lines, would prompt Howe to send the fleet up to Albany in time to bring relief. Pinned down, Burgoyne dug in for a last desperate stand.

Down in New York, General Clinton, left in command of the New York garrison, actually tried a sortie north. In short order he cleared the defenses around the West Point highlands and sailed as far north as Esopus, modern day Kingston, New York. After burning the town on October 3, Clinton turned around and sailed back to New York, convinced he had created a major diversion that would free Burgoyne from his trap. It didn't. Word of Clinton's abortive raid and turnaround was allowed to pass through the colonial lines to Burgoyne. Cornered, out of supplies, and with winter threatening, Gentleman Johnnie surrendered his entire commmand on October 17, 1777.

From start to finish the year 1777 was one good idea after another gone bad for the British. Germain's whole plan, Burgoyne's march through a trackless wilderness, Howe's move to take Philadelphia, even Clinton's strange raid; all seemed like great strategies at the time. They had, however, failed to take into account the fact that the paradigm of war had shifted. This was not a war of the age of the Enlightenment, a game of princes and kings, fighting for limited objectives, control of colonies, or a mercantilistic edge. It was a war of the age of Revolution, a new war of ideology for a new age, and the old rules simply no longer applied.

A month after the surrender of Burgoyne word arrived in Paris that the colonial "mob" had defeated and captured one of the finest armies of the British Empire. It was true that Philadelphia had fallen, but that was merely a city that could be retaken. Washington was still out there, and if one British army could be defeated, so could others. The wheels were set in motion for French recognition of this new government, and the tide of the war had turned. Germain's plan and Howe's execution had lost an empire.

FRANCE GETS EVEN

Revenge at Any Price?
1780 America

By William R. Forstchen

War makes strange bedfellows, and in the case of the American Revolution, it was the age-old rivalry between France and England which motivated the French to enter the war. There's a wonderful irony to the idea of besting England, since the desire for revenge created the United States of America.

Some historians would lead us to believe that the French revolution had already taken place and brother revolutionaries were now extending a helping hand to their comrades thirsting for freedom in America. Revisionist history aside, France's support of the colonial revolutionaries of North America had nothing to do with dreams of liberty and equality. The young ruling class, including the famous Marquis de Lafayette, were devotees of Voltaire, but then as now it was rather chic to embrace radical causes and wander about denouncing their elders and the very system that catered to them in the first place.

French support of our revolution was first and foremost motivated by the desire for revenge.

Only twelve years prior to the start of our revolution, France was viewed as the true archenemy of any citizen of the thirteen colonies. The Americas had just endured the French and Indian War, which had claimed the lives of tens of thousands; with the native population, by and large, firmly lining up on the side of the French. Though France had been expelled from North America by the 1763 treaty that had ended the war, the memories and bitterness of that struggle would linger for a generation.

The loss to the British was harsher for the French than any personel loss could be to the colonists. The colonist might have lost a farm, even a son or husband, but the French court had lost an empire. Total victory in the Americas had actually seemed possible at the start of the war, but now the cherished province of Quebec and the rich trade grounds of the Ohio and Mississippi Valleys, were lost forever. Tens of thousands of Canadians of French descent were now refugees. Fleets and entire armies had been lost in the struggle and the pride of a nation destroyed while the hated Anglo-Saxon Empire off their coast continued to prosper and grow.

Thus, in 1775, news of the spreading rebellion in the colonies was met with delight. In the years between the ending of the last war and the explosion of rebellion, the British crown had spent millions on garrisons, construction, administration, and paying off the debt of the last war. Conversely France, now freed of most of its vast overseas commitments, had actually made a financial turnaround. No one had realized that economically France might have actually been better off without the huge expenditures necessary to maintain overseas outposts. The economic theories of the mid-eighteenth century were all built upon the mercantilistic theory of colonies providing natural resources, manufactured goods being sold back, and high trade barriers against any potential rivals.

No one really saw in the colonial English rebellion a harbinger of things to come. Among French intellectuals and philosophers who populated the court, it was suddenly all the rage to express support for the rabble in arms on the other side of the ocean.

All of these factors were masterfully played by one of the greatest politicians, intellectuals, and propagandists in American history . . . Benjamin Franklin. Arriving at the French court in 1776 as a representative of the revolutionary government, Franklin quickly set to work. Since his government was not officially recognized by the French, he could not be formally presented in court, or meet the king, but a member of the court he was nevertheless. Playing on sensationalism, he would dress in frontier buckskins when attending affairs, or offer concerts on his famed glass harmonica. He also convinced ladies of the court to join him in nude "air baths" and though he was in his seventies, rumor had it that spending a night with Franklin became an absolute must for the ladies in waiting, who went on to speak of his charms and his cause in the salons of Paris.

He adroitly pushed the American line all the time. To the intellectuals he spoke glowingly of the new age of man and the ideals of Voltaire, Rousseau, and the Enlightenment. To the economists he offered the prospect of unlimited and unfettered trade with colonies rich in natural resources. To the nationalists he offered the heady concept of revenge. "We are in the same fight now," he argued, the fight to humble British imperialism. Though left unsaid the implication was always there that here might be a chance to regain Canada and the riches of the Mississippi Valley.

Franklin gave the French much to think about. Other discussions regarding this rebellion were started. Here there might not just be a chance for revenge, but for a renewed empire as well. They expected that once free of England the thirteen colonies would undoubtedly turn to internal squabbles. In that kind of confusion there might very well be a chance to snatch up some extra tidbits, perhaps wrest control of a colony or two. The prospects were limitless. The salesmanship of Franklin, the convergence of numerous and varied motives, all made intervention in the American rebellion seem very promising. More-cautious voices were drown out when word arrived in the autumn of 1777 that the American rabble had captured an entire British army in upstate New York; ironically, not all that far from the very battlegrounds where, a generation earlier, French and British forces had struggled for control. This closed the deal.

They made a treaty of friendship with the revolutionary government and offered covert financial support. The timing of this, starting in February 1778, might very well have saved the Revolution, since a crucial shipment of supplies, uniforms, and weapons was smuggled through the British blockade and arrived at Valley Forge, having a tremendous impact on morale. Several months later war was officially declared between France and England.

By 1780 a major French expeditionary force was maneuvering on American territory, commanded by French officers and supplied from France. Tens of thousands of French muskets, bayonets, uniforms, and accoutrements outfitted American armies on all fronts. Aging French ships of war, such as the famed *Bonhomme Richard*, were transferred to the fledgling American Navy, and French fleets went into action on fronts as far flung as the Indian Ocean and the Caribbean.

As a result, after the British surrender at Yorktown, the war actually dragged on for two more years, with combat now shifted from North America to the Caribbean, the English Channel, Gibraltar, South Africa, and the Indian Ocean. Spain and Holland both entered the war, seeing their chances for vengeance as well. The place that had triggered the fight, the American colonies, became secondary to all the European participants as they maneuvered to gain control of the Indian subcontinent, to take Gibraltar back from the British, and to raid and counterraid colonial possessions.

As for France, the golden ring of humbling their arch rival seemed almost within reach. But, in the final year of the war, they simply blew it. Major defeats of fleets in the Caribbean, off the coast of France, and in the Indian Ocean threw their plans into complete disarray. The Franco-Spanish alliance to take Gibraltar collapsed in a humiliating defeat. Far worse though was the debt . . . mountains of debt. The cost of maintaining well over ten thousand professional troops in the Americas, of clothing and outfitting the American Continental armies, of funding military operations, the maintenance of fleets, the building of ships and, beyond that, the loss of trade as British raiders snapped up French merchantmen, had not just thrown the French government into the red; it had driven it to the edge of complete financial collapse. All of this effort over years had yielded a lot of personal satisfaction, at least at the start, but had not brought one single franc of profit back to the motherland.

Eager now to get out of the mess, the French went to the negotiating table and in January 1783 signed a peace accord with England. It must be admitted that the English had tried to maneuver them into betraying the Americans, especially when the tide of battle overseas had turned back toward the British, but the French had insisted upon recognition and full withdrawal of occupation forces.

Thus did France gain revenge. But at what cost? Louis XVI had doomed himself with this decision. The debt created by the war and the ruinous interest on that debt forced Louis to call together a meeting of the Estates in 1789 in the vain hope of bringing about a much-needed tax reform. What it got him instead was a revolution, led in part in the opening stages by one Marquis de Lafayette. As for aiding Louis, Washington ruled that out, declaring it was in our best interests to avoid foreign entanglements. Louis lost his head due to the debt incurred in America, and France was torn apart by a Revolution.

So, it seemed profitable at the time to help us out and perhaps in return, the rudeness of French waiters to American tourists is a justifiable price to pay.

BLIGH'S GUYS

The Mutiny on Board His Majesty's Ship
Bounty
1789 Two Months Out From Tahiti

by Brian Thomsen

Popular culture has painted William Bligh as a cruel and
sadistic sea captain who inhumanly tortured his crew
until they had no choice but to mutiny. This view is further supported by two later episodes in his life, when a
second ship under his command also mutinied, and when
a New South Wales colony rebelled while he was governor. His contributions on Captain Cook's expeditions, the
superb seamanship that lead to his successful journey of
3,600 miles in an open longboat with the ill-prepared non-
mutineers of the *Bounty*, and his discovery of the Fiji islands, as well as many other exploits of note, are
usually overlooked.

Captain William Bligh will forever be remembered at
the helm of the *Bounty* on her journey from England to
Tahiti to the West Indies, to provide colonial slave owners
with breadfruit plants that would serve as a cheap yet
nourishing food for their Negro slaves. Poor health condi-

tions, strict discipline, frequent floggings and unreasonable work schedules are often cited as driving the crew, under the honest leadership of Fletcher Christian, to commit mutiny in order to assure their own survival. If his critics are to be believed, Bligh got what he deserved by being too cruel in the performance of his captainly duties.

A closer look at the facts, though, indicate that this is probably not true.

Life in His Majesty's navy was not a bowl of kippers for anyone in the eighteenth century. Malnutrition was the norm, and scurvy was widespread. Flogging was the normal method of individual discipline, with three levels of severity: a dozen lashes (which would leave a man's back in ribbons), fifty (laying a man's back bare to the bone), and two hundred (usually considered a death sentence). Close quarters, the lack of female companionship, dangerous seas, and inexpert navigators were all part and parcel of the naval experience. Given all of the above it was small wonder that there was a strict code of behavior expected of all involved, and a severely enforced hierarchy maintained during the entire duration of a voyage (including any time spent in foreign ports).

The voyage of the *Bounty* was in fact atypical because of its lack of severe conditions. According to records, not a single case of scurvy occurred, and even his detractors are forced to admit that Bligh was one of the most able sea captains of the time, and that he was responsible for keeping his crew safe despite the harsh sailing conditions they were forced to endure due to the seasons and normal conditions of the areas that they had to pass through. As to floggings, sources indicate that he flogged proportionately fewer of his crew than any other captain who sailed the Pacific in the eighteenth century. Even venereal disease did not raise its ugly head among the crew (according to the log of the ship's physician) until after the crew had left Tahiti, thus indicating that standard shipboard rules had to have been relaxed while they were in port.

For all practical purposes, it would appear that Bligh, aware of the normal strains of such a voyage from his own experiences serving under Captain Cook, had decided to take it easy on his crew, only demanding the minimum from them in all matters outside of those affecting the safety of the ship and its mission. It would appear that he also strove to break down many of the barriers that existed between a captain and his crew on a social basis. Senior crew (including on many occasions Fletcher Christian, the chief mutineer) were frequently invited to dine with the captain in his private quarters. Given the ship's lack of a purser on its crew roster, Bligh assumed these duties himself, and frequently lent or advanced crewmen (including Christian on several occasions) credit from their pay as petitioned. Finally, the ship's five months in port in Tahiti were far longer than most captains would have allowed, as they preferred to keep their crews out of temptation's reach for as long as possible.

All of these factors combined lead one to conclude that Bligh was in actuality too lax with his crew. The lack of punishment and hardship that seasoned sailors had come to expect had obviously led to a certain decline in their respect for authority, and with this came a lack of confidence in their captain's ability to be captain, despite all practical evidence of his abilities to the contrary. On the outbound voyage, the crew had had it too good, and in Tahiti, they experienced the temptations of paradise.

On the following leg of the journey the men were

confronted with the normal inconvenience of the naval life, after having been spoiled by a relatively easy passage out and a long vacation in port. Part of their living space was impinged on due to the cargo of breadfruit trees, and their rations cut back slightly due to the lack of stores. But because the men were spoiled, they mutinied. The leaders included the minority of the crew who had been flogged and a preponderance of those who owed Bligh and the ship money.

Bligh's good nature and concern for his crew had backfired and, in all probability, facilitated the mutiny.

Later a formal inquiry into Bligh's responsibility for the mutiny exonerated him from all excesses that might have led to the mutiny, with the lone exception of citing him for possibly excessive abusive language.

Had he walked the walk instead of just talking the talk, he might have remained in control of his ship for its entire journey.

NOT STEAMED UP

Fulton and Napoleon
1800 France

By Bill Fawcett

France was virtually the only ally of the fledgling United States during the American Revolution, and when the French had their revolution, based on the same philosophy espoused by the Constitution, goodwill abounded. Even after Napoleon Bonaparte became a virtual dictator, the United States was one of the very few countries that voluntarily recognized the regime. This resulted in the Louisiana Purchase, the War of 1812 (a major demonstration of misplaced pride and incredibly bad timing) and an influx of Americans looking to support or exploit the nation that had supplied our revolution with Lafayette.

Now, Napoleon was an eminently practical leader. He saw the value of what he could use immediately, and had little truck for what he couldn't unless it improved his standing with the French population. In this sense his direct actions created many things we still use today. Tin cans were developed in response to a contest Napoleon held for ways to supply his army on the march. But there was one invention he rejected that may have made all of the difference, a difference that ended his reign with his capture by the British.

An American from Pennsylvania named Robert Fulton was full of ideas that would help Napoleon to spread the ideals of the French and American revolutions to all of Europe. The young and unproven inventor created and tested a design for a submergible boat. Powered by three men cranking a screw, this ship could travel underwater at a depth of twenty-five feet. Designed to sail close to an enemy ship using folding masts and sails, the submersible was to then disappear under the waves and plant a "torpedo," which is what we call a mine today, against the hull of a warship and detonate it.

In 1800 Robert Fulton traveled to Paris and accomplished the difficult task of gaining Napoleon's attention. This was challenging because the First Consul was effectively running both the army and the government of France. Fulton went so far as to spend a substantial sum creating a prototype submarine. This he showed Napoleon in the harbor at Rouen.

The leading land general was unimpressed. At the time he controlled a fleet almost as large as that of England and had the potential to build one larger. He saw no reason to spend any of his cash-strapped nation's money on a new invention. Particularly one that involved the navy, which he consistently relegated to second place among the military.

Napolean's refusal only momentarily discouraged Robert Fulton. He had another idea. Encouraged and financed by the American Minister to France, Robert Livingston, in 1802 Fulton created and sailed a steam-driven paddle-wheel boat up the river Seine at a speed of 3 mph. Which sounds slow until you consider that sailing ships were considered to be fast at 7 to 10 knots even in the best wind. On any river a sail-driven vessel was invariably slowed to a crawl due to the necessity of sailing against the wind on a regular basis. The key element was that Fulton's paddle wheeler did not depend on the wind and could even sail directly into it with little loss of headway.

Napoleon was now enjoying one of the few periods of peace his empire ever enjoyed and, further more, was deeply involved in building up a more professional army. Fulton's request for an interview with Napoleon was refused. He never saw the prototype of ships that could travel against the wind. It may be that they never crossed the emperor's mind again.

A few years later the Grand Armee sat in the ports of France waiting for the combined Spanish and French fleets to break out of their ports and escort them for a landing in England. The French and Spanish fleets sat trapped in their harbors by a British blockade. Perhaps the emperor of France, as he stood in those blockaded harbors, thought about the American artist's underwater ships and wondered if they could have driven the Royal Navy from his ports.

For the invasion of England, a project Napoleon had spent a large part of the budget of France to prepare for, timing was the issue. The barges that would carry the army needed the right wind and calm seas. They also needed to avoid slaughter by the Royal Navy. To accomplish this the French needed two days of control of the Channel. By 1815 Fulton's steamboats were sailing at speeds over 5 mph on the Raritan, Potomac, and Mississippi Rivers, as well as at a number of ferry crossings. Had these same ships been developed in France, which was a much richer nation, it is possible, even likely, that the French army could have simply waited until the wind trapped the Royal Navy in port, a common occurrence, and steamed across the Channel. Once on shore those parts of the British army remaining in England would have been hard pressed, if not overwhelmed. But the combined fleets of France and Spain lost, and the army that had waited for over a year on the Channel shore packed up and invaded Austria.

Over the next decade England would finance virtually all of the resistance to the emperor. After 1805 the British fought France at every step; on the Iberian Peninsula, in Egypt, the Mediterranean Islands, and eventually in France itself. Had Napoleon been able to land any sizable army in England, it is easy to speculate that he would have succeeded in making himself master of all Europe. If he had had steamboats he could have made such a landing. Taking a chance on this new invention, although risky, was probably a sounder move than Napoleon's great plan, which changed the course of history with its failure.

TO GIVE AWAY A COUNTRY

The Mexican Invitation to Austin and Friends 1800s Texas

By William R. Forstchen

This one might not go down well with Texan Nationalists, but there is another side to the Alamo legend. John Wayne and company did not die at the Alamo defending a Texan homeland from foreign invaders. Actually, it was almost the other way around.

After successfully breaking away from Spain, Mexico declared itself a free and independent republic in 1824. At that moment Mexico was, in fact, the largest nation in North America. Its territory stretched from the Yucatan Peninsula in the south, up along the Pacific coast past a tiny mission at San Francisco, across the Rocky Mountains and down into the great prairie. At Santa Fe there was a city already more than two hundred years old, and numerous missions dotted the frontier. And there was precious little else when it came to population.

Of particular concern was the region north of the Rio Grande. It was a vast, unmapped region, where, since the Louisiana Purchase in 1803, there had been an ever increasing flow of freebooters and land grabbers moving outward from the west bank of the river. Even more abhorrant in the eyes of the new republic was the fact that they were bringing slaves with them, a practice outlawed in the Mexican Constitution.

It was evident that sooner or later the pressure on the remote northern border would grow. The only answer was to settle the vast province of Texas first. However, no one in their right mind in Mexico wanted to go. The region was lawless, and the native population decidedly hostile and notorious for the slow deaths inflicted on any who fell into their hands. An American general a generation later would declare, "if God gave me hell and Texas, I'd rent out Texas and live in hell." His statement was even more true in 1824.

Finally it was some Americans who offered a solution that seemed like a remarkably good idea. The Mexican government was approached by a group led by Stephen Austin. Austin pointed out that the great land of Texas was unsettled, and that pressure would grow from the United States over this untapped resource. Why not let some Americans in ahead of any official move by the United States? Let the settlers have land, bring it under cultivation and develop a vested interest in the future of Mexico. Then, if the United States came along, there'd be thousands of hearty defenders, ready to come to arms to defend the Republic of Mexico!

A few major concerns were raised about the offer. First was the morally offensive issue of slavery. Austin and company solemnly declared that any black man who entered Mexico would do so as a free man. This was reassuring to the Mexicans. Second was the age-old question of religion. Austin convinced them that any Americans who came into Texas and acquired land would naturally convert to Catholicism. Their new-found faith would be even more reason for them to want to see a Catholic republic stand against one where anti-Catholic feelings were still quite strong. Lastly all settlers would be expected to learn Spanish.

The government officials of Mexico who believed Austin will forever be an argument against letting anyone into government service without first undergoing a serious intelligence test. The Mexican government opened the doors wide to Austin and his followers.

In less than ten years well over ten thousand settlers poured into Texas, coming predominately from the deep and middle south. Government officials sent up from Mexico to monitor the settlement program were stunned to discover they'd been lied to!

Slaves by the thousands were being brought in to work the new cotton fields opening up along river bottoms near the coast and up in the northeast corner of the territory. And as for Catholicism, most settlers were outraged at the mere thought of having anything to do with the practice of papism. In fact the new "Mexicans" were already declaring that plain old English was the only language they'd ever learn and only "greasers" spoke Spanish.

Well the rest, as they say, is history, at least as written by the winning side. The whole Texas settlement program had proven not just to be a joke, but in truth an outright invasion, with many of the settlers openly declaring that sooner or later Texas would be part of the United States and that was why they were there.

Mexico finally went to war against its rebellious province, declaring all Americans would have to leave if they did not convert and give up slavery. In addition, and this is rarely mentioned in accounts of the Alamo, the Mexican government announced that any slaves who came to their lines would be immediately emancipated. The Mexican army saw itself as the liberator and protector of their native soil, while the Texans loudly declared that it was an army bent on stealing their property and fomenting servile revolt. Film dramas about the Alamo never seem to have a defender shouting, "here's for slavery!" The Mexican army's belief only made things worse. Several massacres ensued, the worst of which was not at the Alamo but several days earlier, at Goliad, where nearly four hundred POWs were summarily executed. The murder of hundreds of prisoners was perhaps just as big a motivator as the Alamo when it came to rallying men to the standard of Sam Houston, the famous Texan general.

Texas became an independent republic, which lasted ten years before they signed a treaty of annexation with America in 1846, thereby triggering what we call the Mexican War. The Mexican War resulted in a wide-scale land grab as Americans swept up what would later be nearly one-third of the continental United States. This in turn upset the balance in the United States government and eventually would lead to civil war.

All because a couple of Mexican bureaucrats actually thought that Austin's proposal would make things easier for them.

CHOOSE THE CAPTAIN WELL

The *Somers* Incident
1842 Atlantic Ocean

By William R. Forstchen

The training of young gentlemen for a career in the navy was a haphazard and often dangerous experience in the navies of the seventeenth, eighteenth and early nineteenth centuries. The usual procedure was for a boy to obtain a commission as a midshipman, usually for a set price, then be assigned aboard a man-of-war. If he was fortunate, or had the right political connections, the lad would be assigned to a captain who had a positive reputation. Hopefully one who looked out for his boys, provided for their education, trained them in the traditions of the sea, and, most importantly, protected them from the worst abuses that were the usual lot of youngsters serving at sea. For the most part, these new sailors had it far worse, facing a superior officer who was indifferent at best to their formal education. The boys were usually subject to the worst of what human nature could produce when rough, violent men were locked aboard a wooden prison.

Our enlightened republic, in the early 1840s, decided to take a second look at how these young men were trained. For over a generation West Point had been turning out superior officers for the army, while the navy focused in on the idea of having an academy at sea, a training ship not just for midshipmen destined for rank, but also for apprentice seamen. The ship would serve as a floating school, cruising the Atlantic and returning after a year's duty with men fit for transfer to the fighting men-of-war of the American navy.

Rather than convert an old brig or schooner, the navy ordered the academy ship to be built from scratch and they came up with a monster. The *Somers* was built along the lines of a brig, a hundred and twenty feet in length, but only twenty-five in the beam. Its lines were sleek, low, more like those of a racing ship or blockade runner than a training school. But it was the room below decks that posed a real problem. The headroom on the lower deck was only 4'10" and it seemed like the designer had planned the ship more for a crew of midgets than a full compliment of healthy, active young men. The ship, at best, had room for a crew of fifty, but by the time it sailed on its first training voyage the compliment was up to over one hundred and twenty.

The naval board in charge of the program cast far and wide for an appropriate commander and finally settled on Commander Alexander MacKenzie.

MacKenzie had over twenty years service at sea and was well known in the fleet for being a writer and for socializing with the literary set, including James Fenimore Cooper, but also for being a stern taskmaster with a strong moralistic streak. He was thus, in the eyes of the board, a fitting choice.

The navy of this time was ruled by men who had served in the War of 1812, where they earned lasting glory for their exploits aboard the raiding frigates that had dared to face the might of the entire Royal Navy. MacKenzie was related through marriage to the legendary Perry, and had served with Decatur, although his own rise through the ranks had been less than noteworthy. Too young to have made a name for himself in 1812, he had passed his entire military career overshadowed by the leaders of that war. Perhaps someone adept at reading human nature might have seen the warning sign, but no one seemed to notice his resentment of his assignment to a diminutive training ship rather than a fully gunned man-of-war.

The crew was fitted out, the recruits loaded aboard, and all was prepared for the first voyage of the navy's new training ship. At the very last minute one extra midshipman was loaded aboard. His name was Philip Spencer, and he was a less than shipshape lad. By the age of eighteen he had already earned a reputation as a rebel, sullen and resentful toward authority and with the earned distinction of being expelled from several schools. He was there for one reason only . . . his father was John Spencer, a New York politico who just happened to be Secretary of War in the cabinet of President John Tyler. John, at wits end with his rebellious son, had taken the suggestion of the Secretary of the Navy, Abel Upshur, that the navy would make a man out of the unruly boy.

The *Somers* cast off; MacKenzie immediately demonstrated his reputation as someone not to be trifled with, ready to jump on any apprentice or midshipman for the slightest infraction. Heading out into the Atlantic they made the crossing to Madeira and from there down the coast of Africa to the colony of Liberia. Below decks life was hell as over a hundred men jammed into a deck area of only a couple of thousand square feet. Philip already had one big strike against him: being the last midshipman aboard he was immediately resented for being yet another extra body, which packed them in even more tightly. Beyond that his manner immediately gave offense. Spoiled, imperious, and unkempt, his attitude and behavior quickly set the others against him.

By the time the ship had reached Madeira, Philip was completely ostracized by his peers. It was at this juncture that he committed a major mistake. He threw his lot in with the apprentice seamen. The navy, like any military system, has always been a class-conscious one. Officers do not mix socially with enlisted personal, not even boys who are in training for those ranks. Philip started to hang out with the apprentices, but far worse, he started throwing money around in an attempt to buy friendships. The apprentices were more than happy to take him into their ranks, but it triggered a running tension between Philip, his fellow midshipmen and the apprentices. Rumors of the tension got back to MacKenzie, but at this stage he didn't appear to do anything, though it was noted that he was increasingly difficult to approach, given to outbursts of temper and denouncements of the entire ship's compliment.

Docking at Monrovia, shore leave was granted. For a group of boys from the farms, villages and small towns of mid-nineteenth century America, Monrovia must have been an exotic place. Philip, upon returning from his shore leave, displayed a very bizarre behavior described as a giddy hysteria. Later historians believe the boy most likely got into the local drug culture and had returned to

ship thoroughly stoned. For an upright sailor like Mac-
Kenzie, the boy's behavior upon his return, and for days
afterwards, drew increasing notice. Philip had turned se-
cretive and there were rumors that he had formed a frater-
nity, or club, with several of the apprentices, complete
with secret signs and cryptic writing. At this time forming
such clubs was a popular pastime.

For MacKenzie, however, something snapped. It was
obviously not rational fear, or even a compiling of credi-
ble evidence that drove him to his next act. A look at the
records, and how subsequent events unfolded, can only
be explained by the conclusion that Commander MacKenzie went insane. Perhaps it was the long years of frustration, the slow climb through the ranks and then being
shoved aside to a third-rate ranking in command of a
training ship. Perhaps it was Philip himself, the spoiled
son of a high-ranking official, that drove MacKenzie over
the edge. It might even have been due to illness contracted on the voyage. No matter the cause, MacKenzie
sank into full-blown paranoia. This paranoia was fed by
a squealer who whispered about Philip's "secret" group.

One night on the return voyage back to Saint Thomas
in the British Virgin Islands, MacKenzie led an armed de-
tachment into the foreward deck, the realm of the apprentice seamen. There he confronted Philip, had him chained,
then strip-searched. Tucked into the band of Philip's hat,
MacKenzie found a strip of paper with what looked like
Greek writing. The captain immediately declared that the
sheet of paper, which disappeared by the time the ship
docked, was actually a list of who Philip was planning to
assassinate in a bid to turn the *Somers* into a pirate ship.
Two of the apprentices were arrested as well, and since
there was no place to put the prisoners the three were

dragged up to the main deck and chained next to the mainmast with an armed guard placed over them.

Whether this conspiracy was entirely a figment of MacKenzie's imagination or was simply an ugly rumor spread by an apprentice or midshipman will never be known. MacKenzie dragged the crew one by one into his quarters, questioning them about the conspiracy, the whisperings to have him assassinated, and most of all what knowledge others might have about additional members of Philip's evil cabal.

His investigation began to ressemble a witch-hunt, as some members of the unhappy crew, seeing a chance to get even with someone or out of fear that someone might try to get even with them, started to point fingers. Eventually fourteen boys were chained amidships as the ship continued its course westward.

MacKenzie, in an ever-growing panic, now turned to his fellow officers, crying that they were all on the edge of disaster. It was obvious that the evil Philip had polluted the entire crew. If fourteen boys had already been discovered, how many more were guilty as well and were now lying in wait for the chance to storm the quarterdeck, kill the officers, and set their comrades free?

For everyone else on board it must have been hell. MacKenzie, as captain of the ship, was the ultimate authority, and the ship was plunged further into chaos as he spun out of control. At this point, the first officer should have arrested him, however that particular man was terrified, not fully sure if he might be the next one to be denounced in the purges. The doctor, who could have declared MacKenzie insane, was similarly paralyzed.

With his terror of imminent mutiny MacKenzie now made his most outrageous demand . . . that all the conspirators should be hanged. The officers resisted. Only a general court martial could pass such a judgement, and only under extreme duress in time of war could a captain summarily execute a member of his crew. But this was duress, MacKenzie cried, pointing to the gathering crowd chained around the mainmast. If the conspirators were not hanged at once, surely the rest of the crew would rise up to free their comrades.

In the end the other officers relented, though they did manage to talk MacKenzie down from a full lynching of fourteen to just three; Philip and the two apprentices first arrested with him. As soon as the officers agreed, MacKenzie rushed to the mainmast, followed by armed seamen carrying ropes. He told them they had ten minutes to live. All three started to beg for their lives and resist the approach of the hangmen. The horrifying result was that the ghastly ritual dragged out for nearly an hour, with the three pleading for their lives, crying, praying, squirming and kicking until at last ropes were tightened around their necks and the three were hoisted aloft, the only sailors in the history of the United States Navy to be executed without trial.

Two days later the *Somers* put into Saint Thomas, the bodies having been cut down and dumped into the sea prior to docking. MacKenzie waited only long enough to resupply and then put right back out again, bizarre behavior for a man who, only days before, was convinced that his entire crew was about to rise up and cut his throat. He sailed straight to New York, with the eleven remaining prisoners still chained to the deck in terror that at any moment they might join their three departed comrades. Once ashore he filed a sealed report to the Secretary of the Navy and the eleven prisoners were taken off (after several months in jail the eleven were quietly released and sent home, the rest of their term of service forgotten).

Needless to say there was a bit of an uproar. First off, the Secretary of the Navy had to inform the stunned Secretary of War that his son had been summarily executed as a mutineer. In the short but brilliant history of the United States Navy there had never been such an incident, nor would there ever be again, and at first government officials and the public simply were not sure how to react.

MacKenzie came out fighting, painting the blackest possible picture of the peril he had so bravely faced down. Beyond that, friends and relatives of MacKenzie in the service rallied to his side. Philip was portrayed to the press as a murderous, drug-addicted villain. Though never stated openly there was also the implication that the son of the Secretary of War was given to illicit vices, a charge that the navy had always been highly sensitive to. The campaign grew so heated that it actually exploded into violence at a cabinet meeting, with the elder Spencer going for the Secretary of the Navy, with the president and other officials having to wrestle the two apart. Given the social customs of the time it seems a miracle that Spencer didn't call Upshur out or simply shoot him out of hand.

A countercampaign finally emerged, started by a mysterious anonymous letter which circulated in the press and is assumed to have been written by John Spencer. It fought to clear the name of young Philip, painting him as a misguided boy who might have deserved a good flogging or two but who was certainly not a criminal, and in turn attacked MacKenzie as a psychotic tyrant not worthy of his uniform. A general court of inquiry was held at

MacKenzie's request. It was packed with supporters and friends, and he was quickly cleared.

This caused even more of an uproar. One of the apprentice seaman had been married and his widow allied with Spencer to bring MacKenzie before a civilian court on charges of murder. This request was tabled by the judge it was presented to since the general inquiry was in session. When the inquiry closed the road was open for the widow's charges to be brought forward, but her efforts were derailed.

Upshur offered a solution to the growing battle of words . . . MacKenzie would face a full military court-martial for his actions, a response which Spencer and the families of the other boys finally agreed to. Upshur promised that the court-martial would prosecute MacKenzie to the fullest extent of the law. When the court-martial board was announced it turned out that Matthew Perry was to be the presiding judge. Perry was the brother of the legendary hero of the Battle of Lake Erie, Oliver Hazard Perry and also the brother-in-law of the accused. What's worse—if the military court found MacKenzie innocent he could not be tried in civilian court due to the rule of double jeopardy.

The court-martial would later be called the trial of the century. It dragged on for months, and agonized over the most trivial details for weeks at a time until everyone was numb. In the end it was a whitewash. MacKenzie was acquitted and there the case died. Three days after that acquittal, the ship's doctor who had gone along with MacKenzie retired to his room aboard the *Somers* and killed himself.

Regardless of the acquittal, however, MacKenzie was considered a pariah. Though the court-martial had acquitted him, it had done so without comment, not adding the usual statement of full clearance that he was "most fully and most honorably acquitted." The only justice was that MacKenzie never again put to sea and was allowed to fade into retirement, where he spent most of the rest of his life writing in defense of his actions.

Our navy has commissioned three destroyers, numbers 17, 175, and 614, USS *MacKenzie*. The official *Dictionary of American Fighting Ships*, however, makes it a point of stating that all three are named for Lieutenant Commander Alexander Slidell MacKenzie, the son of our Alexander MacKenzie, who was killed in action off the coast of Formosa fighting pirates in 1867. The fact that the navy feels it's necessary to point out this detail is statement enough regarding the historical judgement on the father.

As for the idea of a training ship for the Navy's midshipmen? The *Somers* incident had frightened the high command and they were not willing to trust the training of midshipmen to an authority who would be so far out of reach once the ship had cast off. They settled on an idea closer to home, where the high command could keep a better watch over it.

For once, however, a fiasco did spawn a truly great idea in the end. In 1845 the United States Naval Training Academy, safely based in Annapolis, was opened for business.

Great Dred Scott!

U.S. Supreme Court Renders Decision in Dred Scott Case
1857 Washington, D.C.

By Brian M. Thomsen

The Missouri Compromise was an effort by Congress to ease the sectional and political conflicts sparked by Missouri's request for admission as a slave state. The level-headed leaders in Congress were determined that slavery would not tear the United States asunder. The Compromise had several results; Missouri was granted her wishes and admitted as such, Maine was admitted as a free state, preserving the status quo, and guidelines were established to maintain a balance between free states and slave states within the Union of the United States . . . but they never anticipated Dred Scott.

Scott was the slave of an army surgeon by the name of John Emerson, whose tour of duty had resulted in him having to leave his home in Missouri for posts in Illinois and Minnesota for several years in the 1830s. On such assignments, Emerson was accompanied by his slave.

After Emerson died in 1846, various white friends of

Scott, most probably abolitionists, encouraged the slave to sue for his freedom from Emerson's estate due to his prolonged residence in free states while in the company of his master. Scott did so, and initially lost the suit, but then won it on retrial in Saint Louis in 1850. The case was appealed and overturned, and in 1852 Scott was remanded to slavery.

It is notable to point out at this juncture that Scott's freedom was no longer in question as he had been purchased from the Emerson estate by an abolitionist by the name of John Sanford who had more or less guaranteed his future emancipation. Sanford, however, wished to use the suit to set a legal precedent, and since his own residency was in New York, a free state, the groundwork had been set for an appeal within the federal court system, an appeal which would eventually reach the Supreme Court itself. Thus Dred Scott's own stake in the case was now marginal at best, while the suit had metamorphosed into a legal and political hot potato which would eventually bring the nation even closer to war.

The abolitionists' objective was obviously to break the slave owners by making it easier for slaves to obtain their emancipation. They eventually hoped to obtain a Supreme Court decision that would find the entire concept of slavery unconstitutional.

The slave owners had their own agenda as well. Ignoring the issue of slaves as personal property for the moment they argued that the case properly belonged within the state court of Missouri, which had already decided against Scott, and its trial anywhere else would be a clear violation of states' rights.

Certain abolitionist factions within the court (notably John McLean of Ohio and Benjamin R. Curtis of Massa-

chusetts) pressed the case for the federal court's jurisdic-
tion, arguing that Scott had to be freed in accordance with
the Missouri Compromise which, as a federal statute over-
rode the lower state court decisions. The case was tried
in a federal court, as they had wanted, but the resultant
decision wound up being far from their liking or original intent.

In a majority decision (7–2), the court decided
against Scott.

The court also ruled that no black man, free or slave,
was a citizen, and, as a result, that they did not have the
right to pursue any suits in a federal court. Furthermore,
the court ruled that the Congress should not have had the
right to ban slavery in any of the territories because the
Constitution protected people from being deprived of life,
liberty, or property; and slaves, of course, were just
property . . . thus striking down the previous compro-
mises that had been reached on the slavery versus states'
rights issues.

The abolitionists, by overreaching legally, had caused
themselves an even greater setback.

The slaveholders, though victorious, were also dealt a
severe blow in the long run. The decision in the court had
fallen along strict party lines, with the seven Democratic
justices being opposed by the two Republican justices.
Such partisanship galvanized the Republican party, and
may have been directly responsible for the eventual election of Republican candidate Abraham Lincoln to the
presidency in 1860 on an antislavery platform—an election which many historians regard as the immediate cause
of the Civil War.

In the end, the original goals of the Dred Scott case
failed to achieve the objectives of either side. The aboli-

tionists lost their major case for slaves' rights and even suffered a setback in their fight against the constitutionality of slavery, while the slaveholders' immediate victory in court set the groundwork for the war that they would eventually lose. Only Scott himself benefitted. After the Supreme Court decision, Scott's owner set him free as he had promised.

Dred Scott, now sixty-odd years old, would die the following year.

BUY AMERICAN

Colonel Ripley and the English Enfield Rifles
1860 United States

by William R. Forstchen

Colonel James Ripley, West Point class of 1813, may very well have been responsible for the bloody four-year length of the American Civil War, a conflict which might have ended in a matter of months. Sixty-seven years old when he assumed control of the Ordnance Department of the United States Army in 1861, Ripley disdained any innovations proposed for arming the burgeoning armies of the North. Amongst Civil War buffs he is well known as the man who used every bureaucratic means possible to block the introduction of breech-loading weapons for the infantry, especially the rapid-firing Spencer rifle, which he claimed would only encourage men to "waste ammunition, which is expensive."

His greatest folly, however, was not a sin of commission, but rather of omission, and it cost the lives of tens of thousands of soldiers on both sides.

The story begins in 1852 when England sponsored the

first of the modern World's Fairs at the newly constructed Crystal Palace. The American display was opened with nothing more than boxes of machined parts. Volunteers were taken from the audience, and within a matter of minutes guided through the assembling of these parts into a fully functional Colt revolver, a masterpiece of precision interchangeable manufacturing. So revolutionary was this demonstration that the British Parliament assigned a commission to travel to America to unlock the secrets of this new technology, and one of their first stops was at the Springfield Armory, which at this point was just gearing up for mass production of the new 1855 model Springfield .58 Rifled Musket. Awed by this precision capability, the British government purchased a full working factory. Within three years the British began manufacturing their own rifled musket, the .577 caliber Enfield, which was nearly identical to the American Springfield except for slight modifications in the hammer and a three thousandths of an inch difference in caliber.

The advent of hostilities in America caught the federal army completely flat-footed, though some would later claim that Jefferson Davis, Secretary of War under Buchanan, had in fact deliberately sabotaged key decisions for preparation while still in office. The army was less than 20,000 strong, but far more importantly the stockpile of modern weapons which should have existed, was in fact nonexistent. The model 1855 Springfields that were on hand numbered only in the tens of thousands, of which many were in Southern armories. Weapons dating all the way back to the Revolution were all that were available in various state armories.

Three days after the Confederates fired on Fort Sumter, Lincoln called for 75,000 volunteers, and by the end of the summer further calls went out for an additional half million men. The biggest problem facing the Union was not getting volunteers—in fact men were actually being turned away—but rather how to arm them. This was the situation that landed on Colonel Ripley's desk.

First off, Ripley announced that he saw no problem with smoothbore weapons, which had worked well enough for the army he fought with in 1812, but if everyone insisted on rifled weapons, the rifled muzzle loader would be good enough to serve. There was one little wrinkle though: it would take a year or more for the Springfield armory and various subcontractors to manufacture the needed weapons. Any mention of turning to private arms manufacturers to manufacture high-tech repeating weapons was rejected out of hand.

Faced with this dilemma, a staff officer serving under Ripley presented a very simple solution to the crisis: go to England and purchase the needed Enfields from them. They were offering the weapons at rock-bottom prices on a cash-and-carry basis because by this time the British were already considering an upgrade to breech-loading weapons. As a result, the Union army could be fully armed within a couple of months.

Colonel James Ripley, however, went through the roof when approached with the idea. He had once fought the British, and the mere thought of now running to them for weapons was beneath contempt. In addition, Ripley openly stated his opinion that the war would be over by the end of the summer, so the purchase of several hundred thousand rifles would prove to be a total waste; the armies would already be demobilizing by the time the new weapons arrived. Finally he presented the most telling argument of all: that this was an American war and he intended to buy American. Anything less would be unpatriotic!

The staffer retreated from this tirade, mulled things over, and then returned several days later with a far more convincing argument that he knew would win the old man over. Intelligence sources were reporting that Confederate agents were already in England negotiating to buy up every Enfield in stock, as well as contracting for additional production runs.

Ripley again hit the roof, but not in panic. He responded that if the Confederates wanted to buy the damned English guns that was their business and not his. Then he again asserted that the war would still be over before the guns would even come into play, and that American soldiers would go to battle armed with American-made guns. The staffer persisted, finally arguing that for the good of the cause, if need be, the Federal government should outbid the Confederates and thereby prevent them from acquiring the stockpile. The comment was even passed that if Ripley was still so resistant to the use of the Enfields, that at the least the guns should be purchased and dumped into the ocean so the Confederate states couldn't use them.

The staffer was dismissed and ordered never to bring the subject up again.

Three months later, at Manassas, over thirty-five thousand Union troops went into battle, armed primarily with aging smoothbores. Their final assault up Henry Hill came within mere yards of carrying the day and breaking the back of Confederate resistance. That final gallant charge, however, was shredded by the concentrated volleys of Stonewall Jackson's men, armed primarily with newly issued Enfield Rifles that could kill at four hundred yards and were murderous at a hundred yards or less, a range at which the smoothbores of the Union were still all but useless.

Finally buckling to pressure from the administration, Ripley broke down and started to order Enfields, but by then it was too late; the initial stockpile was already in the South. One of the ironies of the war was that the British continued to manufacture Enfields, with both Union and Confederate purchasing agents waiting at the end of the assembly line. In desperation Ripley turned to the Prussians, who were more than eager to sell off their own muzzle loaders since the Prussian army had already converted to bolt-action breechloaders. These muzzle loaders, and additional arms purchased from the Belgians, were almost all condemned as more dangerous to the man behind the gun than to the target in front of it. As to the far more advanced breechloaders such as the Sharps and Burnside rifles, or the highly advanced Spencers, many Union regiments simply stepped around the bureaucracy by purchasing the weapons with their own funds, accepting with a cold, simple logic that their lives on the battlefield depended on superior firepower and they were willing to take money out of their monthly pay of twelve dollars to purchase it, along with the "expensive" ammunition Ripley kept complaining about.

One of the great mythologies of the American Civil War is that throughout the war the Confederate Armies labored under the burden of inferior equipment. This was definitely not true in the first year of the war, thanks to Colonel Ripley. Right up until the summer of 1862 Union troops, especially in the western theater of operations, fought primarily with smoothbores, while the vast majority of Confederate troops were armed with Enfields. Without the Enfields, the Southern cause might very well have collapsed on the battlefields of 1861 and early 1862. If they had been forced to confront a Union army outfitted with breechloaders and been denied access to the Enfield as well, without a doubt there never would have been a Second Manassas, an Antietam, a Gettysburg, or the bloody killing match of the Wilderness Campaign.

His army lost most of their first battles, they were outgunned and outranged by the very rifles he could have bought, he fought change so that the Gatling gun and repeating rifles barely appeared, and more than any other person his decisions may have prolonged the American Civil War for years. As for Ripley himself, who was finally pushed out in 1863, it is doubtful if he ever considered that there was an alternative to his fateful decision or a need to apologize for his gaffe later.

THE MAN WHO WOULD BE EMPEROR

The Maximilian Affair
1864 Mexico

by William R. Forstchen

How an Austrian Hapsburg archduke, backed primarily by French troops commanded by a nephew of Napoleon, wound up as Emperor of Mexico is truly one of the most bizarre stories in the history of politics and warfare.

Since its declaration of independence from Spain early in the nineteenth century, the nation of Mexico had been beset by troubles. Spain made a feeble and unsuccessful attempt at regaining control after the end of the Napoleonic Wars. Civil war ensued until the rise of General Santa Anna (of Alamo infamy) who, in a brilliant campaign, suppressed rebellion and united the country. But in the 1850s rebellion broke out again, with the liberal republican forces of Juárez gaining the upper hand and seizing Mexico City along with recognition by the United States government. It was at this point that Napoleon's French nephew first appeared.

Napoleon the III of France had always lived in the

shadow of his famous ancestor. He harbored dreams of glory, of a return of the empire. But his wife, Eugenie de Montijo, was of the Spanish royal line and therefore, it was to Paris that much of the old aristocracy of Mexico, primarily of pure Spanish blood, had fled, where they regaled their aristocratic friends with tales of the horrible rape and pillage created by the revolt of the peasants.

The center of the Parisian social scene revolved, of course, around Eugenie, who was a powerful political force in her own right. She believed that the' great challenge of the age was to bring about a resurgence of Catholic power to stand against the growing Anglo-American domination of the world. The refugees from Mexico, quick to pick up on a cue, spread stories of the anti-Catholic sentiments of Juárez and his rebels, and the support of the Protestant Americans for the revolution on their southern border. They feared that America would soon gobble up the rest, using Juárez as a puppet, and slaughter all good (and wealthy) Catholics if not stopped. The empress demanded that the emperor help her poor troubled friends from Mexico, hinting at the same time that the glory of France could be expanded into the New World.

When Juárez announced that, due to the economic chaos following the revolution, he would have to temporarily default on outstanding foreign debts, France, Spain, and England allied against him, established a blockade and seized Vera Cruz. The situation was helped by the fact that America was now tied down with its own civil war and could do nothing in response. Spain and England soon pulled out of the operation but the French stayed on and, by late 1862, a French expeditionary force of 30,000 men had landed at Vera Cruz, and captured Mexico City the following year.

Now comes the strange idea. Napoleon was leery of going it alone in America. Though it was obvious that the Confederacy was winning, there was always the chance that the war up north might end, or, worse yet, that Union and Confederate forces might actually find common cause and decide to turn their collective strengths on Mexico (a proposal that was actually floated by several government officials, both North and South in 1862–65 as a compromise to end the Civil War and carve out new slave states in Central America).

Napoleon had to find some other backers. The old Spanish monarchy was related, through blood, to the Hapsburgs of Austria, and it was through this connection that Napoleon III conceived the grandiose scheme of a great Catholic alliance. Thus he approached his fellow emperor, Francis Joseph (who would still be around fifty years later to lead his country into World War I) with the proposal that they save Mexico together. The Spanish-Austrian Hapsburg connection, should be sufficient reason for them to help save Mexico for conservative Catholics. Napoleon even sweetened the deal with the suggestion that Francis Joseph's brother, the Archduke Maximilian, could be set up as emperor of his own country in the New World. Perhaps someday they could make a grand alliance that would one day encompass all of Central and South America, naturally controlled by a joint French-Austrian/Spanish alliance in Europe. With such power the Anglo-Saxons, and the upstart Protestant Prussians to the north, would be brought to heel.

Empress Eugenie was quick to produce witnesses to the barbaric cruelties going on in Mexico, the alleged victims loudly proclaiming that an Austrian emperor, backed up by a French/Austrian army, would be met with tears of joy by the entire population, who were eager to throw off local rule and let a German-speaking outsider have control instead. When one contemplates this plan with historical perspective, one cannot help but wonder what they were thinking.

But Frances Joseph and Maximilian agreed to the madcap scheme. The latter started to brush up on his Spanish, sailed to the New World, and on June 10, 1864, Maximilian was crowned emperor of all Mexico.

To the poor man's credit, he earnestly believed the idea was going to work and threw himself into his new job as emperor. Projects were planned to help the poor, to build schools, hospitals and public works, and he would unite all of Mexico with a benevolent hand.

Meanwhile, out in the countryside, the war was not going well for the combined French-Austrian armies. The army was primarily made up of infantry, burdened down with sixty pounds of gear and heavy wool uniforms, campaigning against guerilla forces who were all mounted. Maximilian's army, in order to try to hold land, was reduced to stringing itself out in hundreds of small garrisons with many escorts needed in order for a single messenger to get through. Juárez could not stand against the heavy infantry, but they could not corner him, especially after he fled into Union-occupied Texas in 1865 and was given a warm welcome. The emperor ruled Mexico City but no other part of the country.

As for Napoleon III's designs on America, they were decided at Appomattox. Within weeks after the surrender of Confederate forces General Sherman, with fifty thousand combat veterans, most of them black troops from the campaigns in Virginia, arrived on the coast of Texas. Sherman taunted Maximilian, urging him to come out for a fight. He also openly trained Mexican revolutionary troops and reequipped them; a number of the black American soldiers, upon being discharged, joined up with the Mexican forces, their descendants still living in Mexico today.

Napoleon III, faced with the threat not only of a war on land, but a fight in European waters against a huge American navy as well, threw in the towel and announced the "Mexicifaction" of the war. By early 1867 all French-Austrian troops were withdrawn. The casualties from combat or disease, numbered nearly half of the expeditionary force.

Maximilian, on the other hand, simply could not let go. Despite his cohort of schemers and plotters, he had a genuine and honest belief in his cause, along with a high personal sense of honor. A small handful of Mexicans had indeed come to his side, and he announced that he could not leave them behind to run off with the rest of the aristocracy. Maximilian sent his family away but stayed on in Mexico City to mount a final defense. Quickly defeated, he was tried and sentenced to be executed. Napoleon, Eugenie, and Frances Joseph muttered the usual protests but were too concerned with the rapid rise of Prussia to try to intervene.

On June 19, 1867, after a reign of just three years and nine days, Maximilian, Austrian emperor of all Mexico, was put against a wall and shot. His neighbor Napoleon, and his grand goal, might not have been worthy of trust after all.

FOR WANT OF A HORSE

Custer's Almost Greatest Victory
1876 Montana

by Bill Fawcett

George Armstrong Custer was a hero of the Civil War. He began his cavalry career during Union cavalry's darkest period. He stood out even among the bold new leaders of that war. He became, and not without cause, the youngest brigadier general in the Union Army. It was a heady time for a young man, more so for one with high ambitions. General Custer was a national figure, and probably had a chance to follow in our nation's tradition of electing its war heroes. Ulysses Grant had been elected president shortly after the war.

When the Civil War ended, those officers who wished to stay in the much smaller army were forced to accept lower ranks. Even so, Custer was a lieutenant colonel and in command of one of the finest cavalry units in service, the Seventh Cavalry. But this was still less glory than the young officer desired. Most of his postwar military actions were small and against foes unable to sustain a long campaign or major battle. This changed, to a degree, in 1874 when gold was discovered on the lands ceded to the Sioux as the Great Sioux Reservation.

The Sioux had already endured, after some violence, the railroad's invasion of their lands. Now miners built the "Thieves Road" and hundreds poured into the lands guaranteed by the government to the Sioux. The Sioux defended themselves, killing perhaps a dozen miners. For a time it seemed that nothing more would happen, then the decision was made to "force the hunting bands back to the reservation." Apparently this was all the excuse the U.S. government needed to invade the Sioux lands. An ultimatum was delivered, which the Sioux did not believe and a virtual war was declared on the tribes in their reservation. Their first real indication of its seriousness was when cavalry stormed through a small Indian village on the Powder River, killing two people and wounding several more.

After the relatively straightforward battles of the Civil War, fighting against the Indians was a frustrating experience for the U.S. Army. The concept of a stand-up battle was alien to the Sioux, their warriors were concerned with demonstrating individual courage and raiding. The result was that it was nearly impossible to bring about a decisive battle. This led to the following battle plan—three converging columns of soldiers. In this way they hoped to force a confrontation, which the U.S. Army was confident it would win. This plan was similar to that which Custer employed in his actual attack—the infamous Last Stand on the Little Bighorn River. This was for the same reason, the need to force the Indians to fight. As it turned out, that wasn't a problem.

After the Powder River Massacre, hundreds of Indian

families converged on Sitting Bull's camp on the Little
Bighorn River. Eventually there would be 7,000 Indians
and almost 2,000 warriors in the camp. The U.S. strategy
had already begun to fall apart. On June 17, Sitting Bull
and his warriors had met and driven back a column under
General Cook on the upper reaches of the Rosebud Creek.
As history shows, Colonel Custer needn't have been as
concerned as he was about getting Sitting Bull to fight.

The problem that cost Custer so dearly was that he
had to sacrifice everything for the mobility needed to
bring the elusive Indian warriors to battle. What seemed
to make sense to the aggressive colonel was to leave behind six weapons that might have changed the entire outcome of the battle. These were six Gatling guns—early
machine guns. Using rotating barrels they were able to
fire hundreds of rounds per minute. So why, if Custer
knew he would face a larger force, did he leave these
weapons behind?

The answer is that Gatling guns were heavy. They
were on caissons just like cannons. Nor was this a weapon
Custer was familiar with. He had seen demonstrations,
but Gatling guns had not been used except by the navy
during the Civil War. Most damning in Custer's eyes was
the fact that inferior horses were assigned to towing the
guns. They were dismissed out of hand as being too slow
to accompany his cavalry.

We have all seen movie versions of the death of the
approximately 250 men accompanying Custer as they are
overwhelmed by the Indians. With several thousand of
their women and children nearby, it is likely that the
Sioux and Cheyenne would have fought, no matter what
the odds or timing. The decision to sacrifice the new firepower was correct in that it accomplished its goal. It did

guarantee contact with the enemy. By leaving the Gatling guns behind, by sacrificing everything for the speed to guarantee a battle he would have eventually had to fight anyway, Custer made the decision that doomed his command. He sacrificed the use of weapons that would have made a decisive difference. In battles by the British against the Mahdists in Africa during the same decade they had proved to turn the tide. But then Custer probably only had a few seconds near the end of his running retreat to regret that stellar decision.

TOO WILDE FOR HIS OWN GOOD

Oscar Wilde Loses Libel Suit and is Arrested on Morals Charge
1895 England

By Brian M. Thomsen

Over a hundred years prior to the U.S.'s "don't ask, don't tell" stance on gays in the military, British society in the Victorian era had already adopted a similar practice as a necessary means of accommodating the fashionable male members of society whose private hobbies and relationships were in direct contradiction to several laws already on the books.

In 1885 a law had been passed, nicknamed the "Blackmailer's Charter," which widened the legal prohibitions against male homosexual acts (only male, as the queen did not recognize the possibility of there being female homosexuals, and none of her ministers felt comfortable disabusing her of this notion). The newly passed Labouchere Amendment broadened the laws to include prohibitions against all "indecency between males," where previously only sodomy had been illegal.

Such laws, however, did little to discourage the exotic

141

practices of various members of the House of Lords, as well as the various literary lights of the time, and those charged with enforcing the law were more than willing to exempt privileged members of the upper class from its enforcement. Effeminate flamboyance was all the rage, and no one was more outrageous than the successful Irish poet and playwright, Oscar Wilde.

Wilde, an Oxford graduate, award-winning poet, and successful lecturer whose tours had included Greece, most of Europe, and even the American West, eventually settled in London where he quickly became a favorite eccentric of the fashionable set. His sharp wit and outlandish oddities of dress even inspired the publishers of *Punch*, and Gilbert and Sullivan, to include caricatures of him in their work. In 1884 he married Constance Lloyd, by whom he eventually had two sons, Cyril and Vyvyan. His family obligations and his dedication to his poetry and plays, however, never got in the way of other more salacious pursuits. Wilde had become enamored of the young Lord Alfred Douglas, nicknamed "Bosie," who was fifteen years his junior. Wilde quickly took him under his wing artistically, while Bosie introduced him to the gay underside of the aristocracy, where the company of young working-class men could easily be obtained for the price of a dinner. The two quickly became inseparable, much to Wilde's detriment as his young companion was even less discreet than the poet/playwright himself.

Wilde honestly believed "that the Treasury (in deference to his celebrity) will always give me twenty-four hours to leave the country" in order to avoid the humiliation of arrest and a subsequent prison sentence. Surely, he thought, the Newdigate Poetry Prize-winning poet and author of such crowd-pleasing plays as *Lady Windermere's*

Fan and *The Importance of Being Earnest,* and of the decadent bestselling novel *The Picture of Dorian Gray* did not
have to concern himself with discretion.

Soon a major problem arose.

Douglas' father was the legendary Marquess of
Queensberry, who at the age of twenty-one had invented
the rules for the sport of boxing which bear his name
today. He didn't approve of the company that his son
was keeping, and strictly forbade him from seeing Wilde.
The son disregarded his father's wishes, forcing his father
to take sterner actions.

As a result Queensberry began a campaign of harass-
ment against Wilde in an effort to publicly embarrass him.
Wilde remained unfazed.

The last straw came when the father left his calling
card at one of the society clubs of which Wilde was a
member. The card's inscription read *"To Oscar Wilde,
ponce and Sodomite."* Wilde was outraged and decided to
bring this campaign of annoyance to an end by bringing
a libel suit against the man.

Wilde's friends and associates begged him to drop the
suit, fearing what might be revealed during its proceedings, but Wilde ignored them, confident that his wit and
superior intellect would take the day. Unfortunately,
Wilde's wit was no match for the bought-and-paid-for testimony of no fewer than ten young hustlers (and less-
than-loyal acquaintances of Bosie) who were more than
willing to cast aspersions on the good name of Wilde,
bringing out into full public view the unlawful acts in
which he had blithely engaged.

Faced with the damning evidence in hand and less
than thrilled with the disdainful manner of Wilde on the

witness stand, the presiding judge quickly threw out Wilde's entire case.

Wilde lost the suit, and within hours of its dismissal, was arrested and convicted on a morals charge using the testimonies from the libel case that he himself had inadvertently brought out into the public. With no ready defense and his friends and allies afraid (or too embarrassed) to come to his aid, he was sentenced and made to serve two years in Reading Gaol for offenses under the Criminal Law Amendment Act.

Wilde had gambled that his position in high society would protect him from the strong arm of the law, and it would have too, but not even the most fashionable members of high society are allowed to get away with flagrant acts that turn private hobbies into public spectacles.

Upon his release, he went to France, attempted a reconciliation with Bosie and failed. He died, heartbroken, in Paris in 1900 at the age of forty-six.

SEA POWERLESS

How to Build a Navy, Lose Friends, Lose a War, and Then Lose the Navy 1900 German Empire

by William R. Forstchen

Some say that it was a seasick American sailor turned writer who started it all. Alfred Thayer Mahan should, by all rights, have gone into the army. His father, after all, was the famous tactician and West Point instructor, Alfred Mahan "the elder," author of *the* textbook on battlefield tactics and instructor for a generation of cadets who would go on to gain undying fame and glory on the battlefields of the Civil War. Perhaps it was the fact that his father was indeed so overshadowing that pushed Mahan "the younger" into Annapolis and a career in the navy instead.

Alfred junior saw some action along the coast of the Carolinas during the war and afterwards was posted to an extensive overseas cruise . . . and he puked his guts out from one end of the trip to the other. It wasn't just the usual two or three days of hanging over the railing; it was the full-blown, no-matter-which-way-the-ship-rolled,

145

going-to-die seasickness. As a true naval officer Alfred T. Mahan was washed up.

He was beached and bounced around to various port duties until an assignment finally opened up at a new facility . . . the Naval War College. When Alfred T. arrived it was nothing more than a dead-end assignment, a couple of beached instructors who were viewed as true oddities, and he transformed it into one of the most prestigious naval institutes in the world. For it was Alfred who went on to write one of the most influential series of book of the nineteenth and early twentieth centuries, *The Influence of Sea Power Upon History*.

The Mahanian thesis was that it was first and foremost sea power that was the deciding factor in the rise and fall of nations. Armies were tied to a snail's pace of movement, were easily contained, and chained by cumbersome logistical tails. A navy, which could be cruising the Caribbean today, in two weeks could be striking deep into the Baltic. By its very nature a navy was a means of projecting power anywhere on the globe. First and foremost by merely having a fleet, a nation became a power to reckon with. At the moment hostilities were declared a navy's primary mission was to first seek out the navy of its opponent and sink it. Once that was accomplished the enemy was on the defensive, its merchant ships hunted, supplies strangled by blockade, coastal cities under threat of bombardment, colonies cut off and eliminated, and eventually the homeland threatened by seaborne invasion . . . an invasion for which the attacker could choose the place and time, while the defender was forced to expend vast resources defending all points.

In short, according to Mahan, if you wanted to be a player in the global game, you had to have a navy.

Ever since the Vienna Conference of 1815 the European powers had found themselves in a unique relationship with England when it came to naval power. It was England's vast armada of ships of the line which had ringed the Napoleonic Empire with a blockade, slowly strangling the emperor and setting him up for the killing blow. With the end of the war a very sensible deal had been struck between friends, and even former foes. England would maintain its dominance of the sea, a necessity in English eyes for it was so completely dependent on the sea for survival. In exchange for this acknowledgement of supremacy, all other nations would have open access; they could even build their own navies, but never should they offer a serious challenge to this vital supremacy.

France had managed to engage in a little naval saber rattling back in the 1860s–80s, first by building the first true ironclad ship, *La Gloria*, which had rendered the entire English navy obsolete in a single day. The English, however, had come back strong with their own building program and, by the 1880s, were leading the way with the building of all-steel ships; interestingly enough built more often than not with high grade steel imported from the Krupps of Germany.

The French had finally abandoned the effort to match the British in capital ships and countered instead with cheap, innovative technology, for a while leading the way in research and development of light torpedo boats, for which the British developed the turbine-driven "destroyer" in response, submarines, torpedoes and mines.

The Germans, the ancient rivals of France, had always viewed this naval rivalry between England and France with vast amusement. Every gun put aboard a French warship was one less gun pointed at their border; every franc spent on a navy was one less franc threatening the Rhineland. In turn the British had always looked to the Germans as a natural ally to contain French expansionism. In short, the mere thought of a conflict between Germany, the new emerging land power of Europe, and England, the dominant naval power, seemed absurd as long as the French inhabited the Earth. While there was a German navy, it was actually little more than a coastal protection service made up of a few light ships which, when they did make a port call in England, were greeted cordially like a wealthy older brother having an impoverished sibling over for dinner.

And then two key events happened. The first was the publication of Mahan's series of books on the roots of power in relationship to naval strength. The second was the ascension of Wilhelm II as Kaiser of Greater Germany. Quite bluntly, Willie was an overgrown child with an ego problem, which some say was created by the bungling of an obstetrician who mangled his arm during delivery. Being thus scarred in a society that was decidedly macho in orientation, he had grown up with a psyche bent on overcompensation. Whatever the psychological background, Wilhelm immediately began to cut an erratic course in foreign policy.

It's ironic that in many ways he was a true admirer of all things English. His grandmother was the legendary Victoria, for whom he held a genuine devotion, and on the night of the old queen's passing he had sat by her side, holding her hand and openly weeping. For his cousin Edward there was a closeness as well, the two often slipping off together for bachelor weekends; and yet down deep there was a growing naval envy as well.

When Mahan's works were first published they gained some small following in the States, an early admirer being a police commissioner in New York named Teddy Roosevelt. Overseas, however, Mahan became an instant celebrity, nowhere more so than in Germany. Wilhelm seized on the book, promptly ordering the acquisition of German rights, then had a publication run produced so that every officer in the Imperial Navy could read it . . . and they were expected to read it. When Mahan went on a European tour he was greeted in Germany like a superstar, the Kaiser insisting that he meet with Mahan so that the American prophet could autograph his well-worn copy.

Germany soon embarked on a naval development program, as did Japan at nearly the same time. Initially Wilhelm declared the German program nothing more than insurance for the protection of local waters. Yet, as Mahan had also declared, a true global power needed a string of colonies around the world to provide natural resources, but just as importantly to provide bases for repairs, telegraph stations for the relaying of information, and coaling stations for resupply. One of the single largest disadvantages of the transition from wind to steam was that the distance ships could cruise had been drastically curtailed. The ability to hoist sail and arrive three months later in the Pacific without ever sighting land was now gone. No modern warship could sustain itself much beyond two or three weeks at moderate cruising speeds, and two or three days of high-speed maneuvers would not just empty the coal bunkers but so rattle the reciprocating engines that a ship had to have overseas bases for repairs and recoaling. The coaling stations in turn now became strategic targets in and of themselves, requiring fortifications and additional naval protection, along with dozens of colliers shuttling in the precious black rock upon which empires were now built.

For Wilhelm at the start of the twentieth century this was the ultimate good idea. England was not really a rival, but national pride demanded a global presence, global presence meant colonies, colonies meant naval protection and bases, bases meant yet more colonies, more colonies meant national pride and yet more expenditures.

Down along the coast of Africa the Germans took over the few third-rate sites not yet claimed in the earlier scramble for power. Initially the British even welcomed this, since France had, throughout the nineteenth century, been their main rival in this area. Out in the Pacific, Germany picked up additional islands, and at vast expense stockpiled them with coal and linked them together by telegraph.

All this meant yet more building so that, by 1904, a few heads were starting to pop up in the British Admiralty, wondering just what the Germans were up to. In that year a new First Sea Lord, Admiral John "Bobbie" Fisher was appointed. British naval design, ever since the introduction of iron and steam, had wandered about down a number of different paths. Fisher, with the eyes of a visionary, saw the direction of the future and, with a spirited aggressiveness that marked his entire tenure, pushed for a new, uniform all big-gun design. A year later HMS *Dreadnought* came off the ways, mounting ten twelve-inch guns. It was the first of the modern battleships.

It was Fisher's hope that *Dreadnought* would serve as a wakeup call to the Germans. It was all right for them to play around with developing their own navy, even to launch a few capital ships equivalent to those ships already afloat, but Britain must and would remain supreme when it came to the latest designs. If that was accepted by Germany there was no need for any concern or future problems between the two.

The moment Wilhelm saw the specs on *Dreadnought*'s guns and armor envy took hold. He immediately ordered his admirals and ship designers to not just match the newest British creation but to exceed it. It stands to the credit of many of Germany's top naval officers that rather than jump on the bandwagon, blinded by the promise of neat big ships and bigger commands, they tried to talk him out of it. The more pragmatic realized that going into an arms race with England was not just a bad idea, it was pure madness. By the very nature of its strategic situation England would have to remain, no matter what the cost, first and foremost at sea, and its army could stand a distant second. Given the threats of France and Russia, Germany, on the other hand, had to remain absolutely dominant on land. Therefore, in the race for precious resources and manpower within Germany, the army would always come first and the navy a distant second. Why go to the effort of antagonizing England when there was virtually no hope of ever gaining the upper hand?

Wilhelm ordered that the program had to go forward nonetheless. German national pride demanded it. To make it even more expensive, the newly completed Kiel Canal was already obsolete for handling the new, bigger ships, and an expensive expansion program was initiated for that facility as well. Thus did Germany embark on the naval arms race with England.

Within a couple of years German dreadnoughts were putting to sea, armed with eleven- and twelve-inch guns.

The French, showing remarkable shrewdness, totally bailed out of the race, sensing that by doing so they would demonstrate they weren't a threat and thereby focus English attention on Germany instead. The ploy worked. For generations the annual British naval war games had focused on a war with France, with operations focusing in the Mediterranean in order to protect the vital trade route from Gibraltar to the Suez, and of course along the English Channel and Bay of Biscay.

By the end of the decade Fisher had shifted the annual maneuvers into the North Sea, a clear statement to Germany that they were training for a confrontation with any fleet that might venture out of the Baltic. Fisher's obsession with preparing for this conflict went so far as to his pushing for a deal with Japan so that the few ships stationed out in the Pacific could be recalled to home waters. Fisher had read Mahan as well, and he had taken appropriate notice of the stunning Japanese victories over the Russian navy in 1904–05. The opening blow would be crucial; the navy that could put to sea first and blockade the opposition would have the upper hand. Above all else the Germans could not be allowed into the North Sea; and beyond that they must never be allowed to occupy Belgium and Holland, thereby gaining ports less than two hours' steaming time from England.

This became the focus of British foreign policy regarding Germany in the final years before the debacle. A very clear message was sent that the territories of Belgium and Holland were now under the protection of England, a rigid warning that most likely would not have been so strong had there been no German navy. The Kaiser, in turn, replied that he had no desires against England, or its territories. All Germany wanted was a place in the sun, national pride, and projection of its power. Thus did the design race continue as well, the 12-inch guns being trumped by 13-inch then 13.5, then 14, then finally by massive 15-inch guns. Paranoia built on paranoia.

In secret the Germans had already laid out the Schlieffen Plan, the blueprint for taking France, and the path to victory was through the Low Countries of Belgium and Holland. In a bizarre half move, yet another good idea, Wilhelm ordered that Holland be kept out of the invasion route, a move by which he hoped to placate England. It was worse than useless, for Belgium would still be crossed, and by taking Holland out of the invasion plan, the German army would be forced to funnel through and around several key Belgian fortresses rather than simply swinging around to the north and bypassing the obstacles.

And finally it all came to pass. As detailed in the next chapter the dominoes fell, one after the other, until finally German troops crossed into Belgium. The British navy, already mobilized, moved to positions intended to block a German naval sortie. But due to the concern about Belgian ports, the moment the first German soldier stepped into one of the Low Countries war with England was inevitable.

During the next four years the German navy only made one serious sortie. Since everyone's eggs, so to speak, were all in one basket, neither side was all that serious about truly closing for a killing match. Finally ordered out in June 1916 in an attempt to break the deadlock, the German navy ran into the British off the Jutland Banks. The battle that resulted was, at best, a tactical victory for the Germans, who sank several more ships than their opponent, but an absolute strategic failure since the German navy withdrew back into the Baltic, never to venture forth again as an aggressive force. The mere fact of its existence, though, had forced England to go to war and later, because of another folly in naval development, America would join in the fight.

The Kaiser had never really grasped the downside of Mahanian doctrine; that if you create a fleet, you will be perceived as a power, but also as a threat. With the defeat of Germany in 1918, the British were so paranoid about the fleet that one of the terms of the armistice was that the German navy must be immediately surrendered, sailed to British waters, and impounded. So, only one time in its entire existence did the German fleet venture into English waters, and that was to anchorages in Scotland after the surrender. The vast sums of money spent, the failed policy, the loss of empire, and the bitter wars to come were symbolized by this final sailing and the final act . . . once Wilhelm's failed "good idea" had arrived at the British base at Scapa Flow, the Germans, in a heroic act of defiance, scuttled the fleet rather than surrender it. As a symbol it seems appropriate.

THE ARCHDUKE GOES
FOR A RIDE

Or How the Dominoes Fell
1914 Sarajevo

by William R. Forstchen

After twenty years of nearly constant bitter conflict, the rulers of England, Prussia, Austria, Russia and the restored monarchy of France desired above all else to avoid another one. But perhaps the plan to make interlocking alliances, established by these powers in the late nineteenth and early twentieth centuries was the most costly folly ever. When the truly surreal decision by the heir to the Hapsburg throne to visit Sarajevo is added you have a recipe for disaster.

The concept of "balance of power" was clearly laid out by the major powers that gathered at Vienna in 1815, at the conclusion of the Napoleonic Wars. Permanent alliances were to be avoided. Far better was the pragmatic approach of balancing, of forming combinations of power to prevent any one state from gaining hegemony over the rest. Over the next eighty years several wars did indeed erupt, such as the Crimean conflict that pitted France and

England against Russia, the 1859 conflict between France
and Austria, and the wars of German unification during
the 1860s. None of these, however, erupted into a lengthy
global conflict, proving the pragmatic wisdom set forth
in Vienna.

The one change to this equation, however, was the
unification of Germany in the wake of the 1870–71 Franco-
Prussian War. Prussia, coming out of the humiliating defeats of the Napoleonic Wars, had embarked on a direct
plan to unify the small and divided states of northern
Germany into a single state, gathered under the aegis of
the Prussian crown. This policy was adroitly master-
minded by Otto von Bismarck, perhaps the greatest European statesman of the nineteenth century, and the father
of the modern German state.

The birthing of this state, however, did come with a
price; the undying enmity of France who had suffered a
humiliating defeat in the 1870–71 war and lost two provinces, Alsace and Lorraine, to the new country.

Bismarck now found himself in a diplomatic quan-
dary. He fully embraced the ideals of the Vienna Conference, yet at the same time he knew that a truly balanced
relationship would never be possible with France, who
would seek the first opportunity to take back the lost
provinces regardless of the threat to world peace, and
push the new German state completely back to the east
bank of the Rhine. He therefore put forth three simple
foreign-policy concepts. The first was, no matter what,
never antagonize Russia. The last time Prussia had faced
both France and Russia, back in the 1750s, Prussia had
almost been destroyed. The second policy was that though
Austria was primarily Germanic, it was never to be embraced too closely. This was because Austria and Russia

had always been rivals in the Balkans, and also because the Austrians were slowly slipping toward anarchy due to the multinational polyglot that comprised the Austro-Hungarian Empire. Lastly, always stay on good terms with England. Germany and England had been traditional allies due both to their shared cultures and their shared disdain for the French. The Vienna Conference had granted the rule of the sea to England with the understanding that, by so doing, all nations would be granted open access. It was therefore foolish to ever offer a challenge to England.

Thus it stood for well over twenty years. The German navy stayed small, just enough to patrol coastal waters. An openhanded foreign-aid policy was established with Russia, to help their neighbor industrialize and keep them friendly. And the erratic Austrians were kept at a distance.

All this collapsed with the ascension of the young Kaiser Wilhelm II to the Prussian throne. Wilhelm had his own ideas regarding foreign policy, and surrounding him was a new, younger generation of Germans driven by nationalism and "colony envy." They felt the time was right for Germany to gain its "place in the sun." Throughout the eighteenth and nineteenth centuries England, France, Belgium, and Holland had amassed lands vaster than all of western Europe. Germany, if for no other reason that national pride, wanted to take its fair share as well.

Their former wariness about Russia and Austria dissappeared. Regarding Russia, well Russia was a primitive giant and there did not seem to be any sense whatsoever in helping it to develop further by sending it aid. And finally there was Austria. Racial identity and nationalistic fervor were running rampant in the late nineteenth century, and the Austrians were indeed brother Germans. The thought of letting concern about France dictate the relationship with a southern neighbor was an insult.

Wilhelm, feeling that it was time, struck swiftly after ascending the throne. Within a couple of years Old Man Bismarck was out. Foreign aid to Russia dried up, a new building program for the German Imperial Navy was announced, colonization efforts in Africa and on remote islands in the Pacific were launched and closer ties with Austria were sought. Wilhelm's bold program was embraced by flag-waving Germans as necessary for national pride. In 1907 he pulled a remarkable sleight of hand, conning Russia into ignoring the Austrian grab of Bosnia and Herzegovina and further Austrian expansion into the Balkans, then turning around and shafting the Russians when he snuck out of his promise to back their efforts to take Constantinople. Again, everyone cheered. He embarked on a new naval program, promising to match England ship for ship and show the German flag on all oceans. By 1908 the yearly British naval maneuvers shifted their emphasis from planning for a war with France and instead moving into the North Sea and rehearsing manuevers against Germany. But still, the Germans rejoiced at this newfound respect.

By 1910 the dominoes were set up. The old system of balance of power was forgotten. The French, still thirsting for revenge after thirty years, led the way, negotiating secret agreements with Russia, and in turn Russia made pacts with the small country of Serbia. Germany secretly gave Austria an understanding of an "open hand policy," a go-ahead that no matter what mess Austria got itself into, Germany would back it up. England, for their part, let it be known that it had understandings with Holland and Belgium, and if any invader dared to take the eastern shore of the North Sea, Great Britain would sally forth.

Even Japan got into the show, making a pact with Britain to protect British interests in the Pacific. All that was needed now was for someone to topple the first domino.

Thus we come to 1914, and the state visit to Sarajevo, the logic behind which will never be known. Seven years earlier Austria had snapped up Bosnia and Herzegovina from the tottering remnants of the Ottoman Empire, without a fight. The province, then as now, was an insane hodgepodge of rival ethnic groups: Serbs, Croats, Slovenians, Albanians, and Bosnian Moslems. The small nation of Serbia bordered the province on the east. A semiautonomous state under the old Ottoman system, it had gained its independence and now turned to its fellow Orthodox Slavic big brother, Russia, for support. Russia was more than willing to use Serbia as a bulwark against Austrian expansion.

Internally Serbia was in upheaval as well, torn by bitter power struggles, and its own radical groups, such as the Black Hand, which believed that it was the destiny of the Serbs to rule the Balkans. But even so, the Austrians actually thought it would be good to stick their noses into this region, ignoring the fact that their country was also a conglomerate of dozens of ethnic groups. The army alone had to contend with several different languages and dozens of dialects within its ranks and now wanted to add still more turmoil.

The old emperor, Francis Joseph, who had sat on the throne for over half a century, was out of touch with the political realities of his realm. The situation was made

worse by the heir, Archduke Ferdinand—aloof, intellectu-
ally challenged, and a poor communicator. He eagerly
went along with the plan to visit Sarajevo. Rather
strangely, state security received numerous warnings that
various Bosnian nationalist terrorist groups were planning
a hot reception, but somehow the warning never really
got down to Ferdinand. There are some who claim that
poor old Ferdinand was actually set up and the hope was
that he would indeed be shot at, thus providing an excuse
for war with Serbia.

Arriving by train in Sarajevo, Ferdinand and his wife
climbed into an open touring car and started driving
around the city, heading for a meeting at city hall. The
terrorists, the Black Hand organization, were indeed waiting. Obtaining a map of the parade route, the group divided up responsibilities, some of them toting bombs, the
others pistols as they went to their assigned stations. As
the motorcade passed on its way to city hall, one of them
actually lit a bomb and threw it . . . at the wrong car. It
went off, injuring several members of the entourage and
spectators. Bizarrely, Ferdinand insisted on continuing the
tour. As the motorcade pressed into the center of the city
one of the terrorists, Princeps, stood several blocks away,
because some of them had been given wrong directions.
He was actually standing alone on an empty street corner,
waiting for a parade that would never come!

Ferdinand arrived at city hall, wandered about, shook
some hands, gave a short speech and then headed out,
mission accomplished. Ferdinand's driver now became
confused and actually took a wrong turn. Realizing his
mistake he stopped, then backed into an alley to turn
around. Princeps, still lost and disappointed that glory
had eluded him, came wandering by at that moment and

found himself staring right at his target, stopped only a few feet away. Pulling out his pistol he emptied it into the chests of Ferdinand and his hapless wife.

And now twenty years of built-up tension all came crashing in. Austria had its excuse to challenge Serbia. Whether it was a cynical setup or not will never be known, though it should be remembered that Ferdinand was shipped home and received a third-rate funeral, hardly the sendoff for someone supposedly worth fighting a war over. Serbia turned to Russia for Pan-Slavic support. Russia weighed in and Austria now turned to Germany for fulfillment of the "open hand" policy of support. Thus Germany got dragged in and challenged Russia to back off. Russia now turned to France, which had quickly jumped into an alliance with Russia once Wilhelm had closed the money pipeline. Germany, knowing that France would support Russia, now launched its attack on France, but had to cross through Belgium to do it, thereby catapulting England into the fight. The only one with common sense, at least for a little while, was Italy, which ditched its alliance with erratic Austria and sat out the conflict for the next year.

The noble ideals of early twentieth century foreign policy created an inferno that consumed tens of millions of lives, shattered the dynasties of Austria, Russia and Germany, and thus set the stage for the rise of communism, fascism, World War II, the Cold War, and the Nuclear Arms race.

OF CLOCKS, OYSTERS AND POLITICS

The Pollen Clock and British Gunnery Control in World War I
1914 Britain

by William R. Forstchen

Unlike most fairy tales and romance novels, the history of technology, especially military technology, is replete with incidents where the good guy fails to win.

In the nineteenth century naval technology had taken a quantum leap forward with the introduction of three crucial innovations: steam power for propulsion and auxiliary power within a ship, rifled guns and explosive shells which instantly rendered all wooden ships obsolete, and iron and steel armor as a counter to the new heavy-caliber guns. The new paradigm became the balancing of gun caliber, the thickness and weight of armor to defend against comparable guns, and the engine power needed to move the ship and achieve maximum speed. Sailors who had entered the British Royal Navy and made their first voyages with a wooden deck beneath their feet and canvas overhead in vessels almost identical to the ships of Nelson and Drake, would finish their careers aboard

modern dreadnoughts, powered by oil-fired steam tur-
bines and in many ways identical to the battleships only
recently retired from the United States Navy. The nineteenth and early twentieth centuries were without a
doubt the most innovative period in the history of naval
design.

When it came to the application of steam technology
to ships nearly everyone involved was quick to grasp the
ship design, technological, tactical, and strategic changes
created. The wind, which had been all-important, was
now meaningless except for the smoke of battle and visi-
bility. Engineering became all-important as a field of
study, and strategic concerns now included distant bases
fully equipped with modern shops for refitting worn engines, coaling stations for resupply and, by the early
twentieth century, interference in Middle Eastern politics
to insure the flow of oil.

All this attention was focused on the new designs and
changes, but hardly anyone grasped one all-important
consideration, and that was gunnery control. Since the
days of Drake, gunnery control was simply a matter of
presenting a broadside so that your maximum number of
guns could be fired, gauging the distance with your eye,
and timing the order to fire with the roll of the deck so
that your broadside didn't result in an embarrassing
splash a hundred yards short of target.

By the time of the American Civil War ships on both
sides carried weapons capable of firing four to five miles,
but nearly every encounter was still fought at a range
of a quarter mile or less. The weapons were simply too
cumbersome to shift around and aim much beyond that
distance. A few theorists did sit up and take notice of the
results of the Battle of Manila in 1898, when the American

navy trounced the Spanish Pacific Fleet. The Spanish throughout most of the fight had remained anchored in the harbor. The action opened at a range of several miles. Thousands of shots were fired, with the American fleet closing to almost point-blank range by the end . . . and less than three percent of the shells hit.

Quite simply the technology of the weapons and the range they were capable of had far exceeded the training and, most of all, the technology needed to correctly aim them. At a hundred yards a modern six-, eight-, even ten-inch gun could be aimed over open sights, in the same manner that an eighteenth century twelve pounder might be aimed. At a hundred yards they might very well hit the target if the seas were relatively calm. At a quarter mile, firing from even a slightly rolling deck, it started to get a little more dicey. At a mile it would be downright difficult, and if the battle was being fought in ten- to fif-teen-foot seas with the deck rolling and pitching, only a truly lucky shot would score. What was troubling though was the realization that the modern guns now being fitted aboard ships were capable of hitting at twelve, even fif-teen thousand yards, a range where the target would be little more than a speck bobbing around on the tossing sea. Theorists now came to a startling conclusion. No mat-ter how much was spent on a ship, or its armor and guns and engines, if an opponent could somehow unlock the technological secret of how to hit at such ranges, he could totally destroy a stronger opponent before effective over-the-sight range had been reached. This thesis was demon-strated when the Japanese completely shattered the czarist navy at the Battle of Tsushima in 1905. It was felt that technically some of the Russia ships were superior to the Japanese, but through rigid training the Japanese had worked out a basic but effective gunnery-control system. Using superior optics they were capable of judging the range to the Russian ships and, working from a primitive firing table, instantly calculate the necessary elevation of their guns. Observers spotted the fall of shells, then walked them into their target. The Japanese had actually pulled off a hit at 6,000 yards, a remarkable range for that time, though at the climax of the action they too had to close to near point-blank range to finish their opponents off. If only the Russians had been capable of hitting at 8,000 yards. . . .

Enter Arthur Hungerford Pollen. Arthur, a genius for working out complex technical problems, had married the daughter of the CEO of the Linotype Company, England's leading manufacturer of newspaper printing equipment. Now, in 1900, the year Arthur's quest got started, Linotype machines were one of the most complex industrial tools ever devised by man. Having thousands of moving parts, it was a huge typewriter with hundreds of keys hooked to an electrical furnace that produced boiling lead. The lead was funneled by the typist into molds that produced type which was then mechanically set into plates, which in turn printed the paper before being recycled back into the boiler.

Pollen, taking a brief vacation in February 1900, went to visit an uncle down in Malta, and while there went aboard the ship of a cousin serving with the Royal Navy. Pollen was offered the chance to observe the cousin's ship, a light cruiser, engage in target practice and, fascinated, he stood on the bridge, watching as the ship's 4.7-inch and 6-inch guns splashed the water around a target 1,500 yards away. By pure coincidence, on that same day, Arthur had read an article in the *Times* about how British naval units were dismounting 4.7-inch guns, taking them ashore and using them with great effect against Boer positions in South Africa at a range of 8,000 yards. As a naive civilian he asked the innocent question of why could a 4.7 shoot only at 1,500 yards at sea but hit at 8,000 yards on land. Undoubtedly he was greeted with good-natured smiles, a shake of the head and an "ah, my good man, there are difficulties you know . . ." response. He left that day determined to figure out how to give his navy the best gunnery system in the world.

As far as good ideas go it all but destroyed his life.

Returning to England he convinced his father-in-law that it was their patriotic duty (and also a sound business investment if it should work) to launch into a gunnery control R&D program. Given the complexity and precision needed to manufacture linotype machines, Arthur felt the firm was up to the challenge.

Next he set up a hypothetical question which they would attempt to solve mechanically. The question presented was that two ships were ten thousand yards apart, closing at full speed but their courses set fifteen hundred yards apart. What calculations would be necessary for a six-inch gun to consistently hit throughout the closure to target and after the two ships passed each other, with their closest point being fifteen hundred yards apart?

It was shown that on the first shot the flight time of the shell would be thirty seconds, but in that interval of time the range between the two ships would close by 900 yards and, in fact, the gun would be reloaded and capable of firing again . . . with a whole new set of calculations being needed since flight time and height of trajectory had changed as well. In addition, the ships would not actually be closing in on each other at a consistent rate of speed. In fact, the rate of change for distance would be variable as the relative angle between the two ships changed. (If it sounds complex, it is!) Beyond that wind speed, relative humidity, barometric pressure, air temperature, the changing density of the atmosphere the higher the shell arced, heat expansion of the gun barrel, the forward momentum of the shell imparted by the movement of the firing ship, along with the pitch, roll, and yaw of the firing ship would all have to be factored in as well. Though not approached initially, greater ranges would even have to take into account the curvature of the Earth and the Coriolis effect of the Earth's rotation on the flight of the shell if the target was at a different latitude.

The task, given the technology of the time, seemed impossible and in fact was impossible. A group of mathematicians, sitting in the bowels of a ship, each one assigned a single variable, might have been able to work out a firing solution, and by the time they arrived at it the target ship would have passed over the horizon and made it back to port in time for a night's leave for the entire crew.

This didn't stop the undauntable Arthur Pollen. The technical answer was to devise a machine, a calculating machine which would accept the various data inputs provided by observers who would optically measure the distance to the target and its course. Next the relative position and course of the firing ship would be fed in along with data from all the other variables such as temperature and wind direction. This machine, or Clock as Pollen called it since it did look a bit like a clock due to all the gearings, would then provide an instant plot for the elevation and aiming of the guns, which would fire through an automatic trigger when the deck was level. Observers would call in the splashes, adjustments would be made and finally the entire process would synch up, the clock calculating the next firing solution before the shells from the previous salvo had even hit. Once this was achieved the system would automatically fire as fast as the guns could be loaded. It was, in fact, an electromechanical computer.

By 1904 Pollen had worked up a basic design, and now the warning of his cousin that he was crazy to pursue the idea started to prove true. When Pollen first approached the navy with a request for a ship to begin preliminary testing he was met with disdain. He was still a youngster, only in his thirties; his total experience at sea had been a one-day cruise, and though not directly spoken of he was, of all things, a Catholic, far outside the inner social circle of the navy and the contractors who supplied His Majesty's fleet.

Pollen countered by turning out a couple of pamphlets describing the problem of gunnery control and his solution, an effort which was worse than useless since the articles were so complex as to be all but unintelligible to the admirals who were the intended audience. Pollen increasingly seemed like the typical civilian eccentric running around with mad proposals about underwater ships, ships that would launch aeroplanes to sink other ships, and rockets that could be guided by radio beacons.

Surprisingly, Pollen finally got through to the First Sea Lord of the Admiralty, "Bobbie" Fisher. Perhaps because Fisher had come up as an outsider as well he showed a tolerance to listen to Pollen's mad scheme, allowed him to go ahead and use a few ships for testing, and was so impressed with the preliminary results that he ordered an official board to study the system and acquire it as soon as possible. It seemed like Pollen's quest to convince the navy about his good idea had finally been successful. Then along came Lieutenant Frederic Dreyer of His Majesty's Navy.

There always seems to be a Dreyer in a story like this.

Dreyer studied every detail of Pollen's clock, was allowed to examine the intricate internal workings, took copious notes, made a point of befriending Pollen and taking him out to dinner, then snuck off and knocked out a replica of the system. Given the fact that Pollen's system was built prior to vacuum tubes, let alone transistors, the linotype maker turned gunnery-control expert had to rely on a remarkably high degree of precision for his mechanical device to crank out accurate plots. Let this precision slip ever so slightly and the calculations were off. It was much the same problem faced a hundred and fifty years earlier by John Harrison in his quest to build the first chronometer, for which tolerances of tens of thousandths of an inch had to be achieved. Predictably, Dreyer's knockoff was a pale imitation of Pollen's, lacking the precision manufacturing of the true original.

In addition, Dreyer secretly formed a company to turn out his own version of the clock, and doctored up papers to make it look as if he had been researching along the same lines as well. The following year Dreyer helped to oversee a test of Pollen's clock, but unbeknownst to Arthur, Dreyer had his own system installed on another ship participating in the exercise at the same time. In a remarkable conspiracy, the entire test was rigged. Before it was halfway completed the judges declared that Pollen had failed to deliver as promised, and that the new Dreyer

Clock, which just happened to be out there at the same time, had outperformed Arthur's design. What is even more remarkable is that Dreyer was supposed to be present at the tests as an impartial judge working for the Royal Navy, and was one of the referees who called an early halt before a full and fair test had been completed. The questionable ethics of a competitor for a government contract also serving as an officer and judge in the trials didn't even seem to be a concern. Those involved would surely serve well with certain government officials today.

The appropriate reports were submitted, Pollen's good idea was dismissed, Dreyer landed the government contract, patents were given to Dreyer who proved he had begun his research first, and the entire affair was completely covered up. Thus are good ideas converted into government contracts.

There is an even more tragic coda to the tale. Poor Arthur refused to be bullied into silence. Going back to the drawing board he decided to come out with an even better design, one so vastly superior to the ersatz Dreyer model that Pollen would still come back and win. Several years passed as he tried to battle Dreyer while, in secret he worked up a superior design. Unfortunately for Pollen he found an ally in the controversial Admiral Lord Charles Beresford. Beresford was a remarkably dynamic and charismatic figure. He was also a bitter foe of the First Sea Lord, Bobbie Fisher. Pollen had allied himself to the worst foe of the man who needed to be sold if a reversal was ever to be gained.

Finally, in late 1909, through Beresford's influence, Pollen managed to gain a second grudging chance, as much as anything to shut him up, for the navy was now committed to the Dreyer system. Assigned to HMS *Natal*,

Pollen loaded his equipment aboard and started to install it. The captain of the ship was Frederick Ogilvy. Here at last was an honest decent man, who placed the best interests of his country and his navy foremost. Ogilvy, who had always been fascinated with the technical side of gunnery, absorbed every detail of Pollen's machine, not with the intent of robbing him but rather to give it the best possible chance of success. The two became instant friends and allies for the common cause of seeing that Britannia would always rule the waves.

The test was a stunning success. Pollen's latest clock completely outperformed Dreyer's. By the time they had returned to port Ogilvy swore his undying support for Pollen's system and promised he would use all his influence to reverse the unfavorable view of the Pollen system currently held by the admiralty. As if fate was not only opening a path but making sure by turning it into a six-lane superhighway, Ogilvy learned upon his return from the trial run of Pollen's latest system that Fisher had just promoted him to command of HMS *Excellent*.

Excellent was not actually a ship, it was the land-based school for naval gunnery. Whomever commanded *Excellent* had the bully pulpit, being considered the navy's foremost expert on the latest theories of gunnery control and technology. Ogilvy promised that Dreyer would soon be out and Pollen in, and never would a foe dare to stand against a royal ship carrying a Pollen clock.

Ecstatic that his long journey seemed finally at an end, Pollen ordered up champagne and a bucket of oysters to be delivered to Ogilvy and his officers to celebrate the promotion, and happily returned to his home to await the news that he had been vindicated. A couple of days later Ogilvy and his staff collapsed and were rushed to the hospital . . . Pollen's oysters were loaded with typhoid! Within a month Ogilvy was dead. Pollen had managed to poison his one great supporter, who could have turned the tide and an anti-Beresford (and thus anti-Pollen and pro-Dreyer) officer took command of *Excellent* instead. Ogilvy's final report, really nothing more than notes since he hadn't had time to write a full and formal report, now carried no weight and Pollen was pushed off to the sidelines by supporters of his rival, who were loudly proclaiming that Dreyer was the genius of the age.

Pollen's good idea had all but destroyed his own life and another good idea, a friendly gesture, had killed his greatest champion.

Six years later the Royal Navy went into action at Jutland. Battle was opened at a range of sixteen thousand yards, though the ships were capable of firing at twenty-four thousand yards. The British consistently missed, all except for one ship, *The Queen Mary*, which was outfitted with a Pollen system that had somehow been purchased prior to the war. (A standard practice in such a situation is for the government or business firm to finally buy a couple of items from the ripped-off inventor simply to shut him up.) In the opening salvos *Queen Mary* slammed three, perhaps four shells into its opponent while the next-best-hitting ship, outfitted with a standard Dreyer clock, scored only twice. Unfortunately there was no after-action report from the gunnery officers, or for that matter from any officer on board . . . *Queen Mary* took a direct hit and simply disappeared in a blinding flash. In the confusion of the battle the Germans were able to withdraw, having sunk more than they lost, and the war would drag on for two more years.

In 1925, after years of court battles, an aged and

beaten Pollen finally received a 30,000 pound settlement from Dreyer's company for patent infringements. Dreyer retired after a long and fruitful career, heaped with honors, as a vice admiral.

COURAGE OVER FIREPOWER

Fighting the Last War, or Maybe the One Before 1914 British Expeditionary Force

by Bill Fawcett

Rapid-fire weapons were developed in 1870, when the French came up with the Mitrailleuse, and Gatling created his eponymous gun in the United States. The English army quickly took an interest in these rapid-fire weapons, but blindly failed to adopt them. It was a decision that would cost thousands of lives in World War I.

In 1871 a committee was formed by the British War Office to determine the value of the new, rapid-firing weapons. The results were unambiguous—manpower could, for the first time in history, be replaced with firepower. Until this time there was a one-to-one ratio of man-carried weapons to men. The only weapon that could be fired on the battlefield that caused mass casualties was artillery loaded with canister. But even breech-loading cannons required nearly a dozen men and as many horses to crew. The message was timely and its importance obvious, and several wars have shown it to be an accurate assessment. It was, of course, completely ignored.

The arguments against the use of machine guns were just too persuasive. The most significant in the opinion of the War Office was that these new weapons would require excessive amounts of ammunition. Furthermore, it was concluded that machine guns were too heavy for mobile warfare (remember Custer?), too expensive, and too mechanically complicated. Perhaps the most damning conclusion was that the machine gun was too defense oriented and would discourage the "offensive spirit" that every general in that era valued over all other military virtues. Ignoring his own commision, John Adye, the Director of Artillery, stated that these rapidly firing guns were of such limited use that they would be rarely employed. If this were the case, they would only take up baggage space that could be used more productively.

The Boer War showed the losses that an army would take attacking entrenched foes that didn't have machine guns. Rather than see how this would change the nature of the battle and make machine guns more important, the conclusion was reached that the machine gun wasn't needed since ordinary firepower could do so much damage. Then came the Russo-Japanese War and the massed Japanese attacks against entrenched Russian positions around Port Arthur. There had been a large number of machine guns on the Russian side, leading the War Office to conclude that machine guns were not decisive, even in defense. What the European powers far from the battles had failed to note were the massive losses suffered by the Japanese. They even began to look favorably at the bayonet, as defense against the Japanese-style self-sacrificial attacker.

Not all officers failed to see the value of the machine gun. The visionary captain J. F. C. Fuller wrote an article in the "Tactics of Penetration" on which he discussed at some length a scenario that predicted the 1914 German offensive tactics amazingly well. Still, the conclusion that pure courage and a determined bayonet charge could overcome any machine-gun and rifle defense prevailed amazingly far into WW I. It should have been washed away at Loos, where the cream of the British army advanced in neat columns of four into the barbed wire and machine-gun fire. Almost 80% of the men attacking were killed or wounded. There were no casualties on the German side at all. This should have made the point so strongly that anyone could get the message. Amazingly this wasn't the case. As much as a year later Sir Douglas Haig wrote to the War Office that the "machine gun is a much overrated weapon, two per battalion is more than sufficient." Training practices reflected this bias and what machine guns were produced in 1915 often sat idle for want of trained officers while men attempted again and again to advance into machine-gun fire with fixed bayonets. The premise that courage could overcome firepower faded slowly and was really only defeated after over a million men had died on the altar of offensive spirit. Courage is a necessary part of a good soldier, but placing it above common sense and rapid-fire weaponry sounded right only to the commanders who sat far behind the lines during World War I.

FOR THE GOOD OF THE EMPIRE

Czar Abdicates to Avoid Bolshevik Revolution
1917 Moscow

By Brian M. Thomsen

"A change of faces and not only faces but the whole system of government is imperative . . . Your excellency, we are on the eve of great events whose outcome we cannot foresee . . . everything tells me that you have already selected the most dangerous path—disbanding the Duma. I am convinced that before three weeks are out a revolution will ignite that will wipe everything and you will not be able to rule."

The time of revolution had come to a Russia wounded and disheartened by war and widespread economic depression. Czar Nicholas II was being advised by his consuls that he should step down in favor of the Duma. If the "tyrannical czar" (as the Bolsheviks saw it) was removed, the people's parliament, the Duma, would be able to step in and remove the threat of revolution by defusing the crux of the Bolshevik argument.

However, Nicholas had never really thought of him-

179

self as an iron-fisted tyrant like the czars before him. In 1905 he had finally given in to the liberal voices from the West and diluted his own autocratic powers by establishing a national elected parliament, the Duma, and legalizing opposition political parties and trade unions. At the time he thought his Russia would survive through necessary compromise.

By February 1917, bread shortages, strikes, lockouts, and demonstrations in the street led everyone to believe that Russia was at the brink of anarchy. The military high command realized that it had two choices—send in fresh troops to try to settle the civil discord with force, or seek a political solution by working with the Duma. They chose the second option, and the Duma graciously proposed a solution of its own.

The czar must abdicate, they proposed, and the ruling power must be given to us. This will quell the revolution.

The proposal was conveyed to Nicholas, who was initially against it and threatened to dissolve the Duma, but he was eventually made to see their point of view, and on the twenty-eighth he abdicated rule for both himself and his son, ending the Romanov rule of Russia.

The Duma knows what it is doing, the former czar thought. They will save my Russia.

Nicholas was reunited with his family and put under house arrest, having been assured of protection by the provisional government of the Duma. Not only was Russia no longer a monarchy, but the Duma was then dissolved in favor of an amorphous assembly made up of former members of the Duma who had basically engineered the coup with the military high command. Nothing could stand in its way . . . except the Bolsheviks, of course, but they were a disorganized lot in search of a leader.

The Duma had made a few critical mistakes, and were soon made to suffer because of them.

First, they had really begun to believe their own press, that is, that they were the people's parliament, and worse than that, they actually thought that the masses believed this as well.

Second, they honestly assumed that Russia needed further liberalization, and that it had to become more like its constitutional cousins in Europe. In reality, the autocracy of the czarist government had made Russia thrive. The hated tyrant czars of the past, like Nicholas I and Peter the Great, had also been among Russia's greatest leaders. Under the czar, the peasants groused and complained . . . but they obeyed since they never realized that they had a choice. Years of the monarchy had made the masses secure about their place in society. Without a czar in place, everything was up in the air. No one knew who to obey.

Thirdly, and most critically, the former Duma members didn't have a plan. They had assumed the power, but did not know what to do with it. As a result it began to dissipate and a power vacuum formed that the Bolsheviks were more than willing to use to their advantage. In April of the same year, Lenin returned to Russia and began to fill that void, and in October of the same year, the Winter Palace, where the so-called Provisional Government was in session, was surrounded and ceded to the Bolsheviks. The Duma's solution had been a temporary one at best, and as its less-than-six-month run proves, a fatal mistake in the long run.

Nicholas II had ceded his power, had lost the Ro-

manov hold on Russia, but had been promised his safety
and that of his family by his successors. But Russia was
on its way to becoming the Soviet Union, a socialist state.
The revolution that he had been assured could be avoided
through his abdication was now in full force, and all previous assurances were worthless.

Nicholas and his family were sent to Siberia and then
to the Urals, all the time still under house arrest. During
the entire period after his abdication, the former czar had
resigned himself to the oppression of the peasants that his
predeccessors had made much use of.

He was even powerless to ensure his and his family's
continued existence. In July of 1918, an order came down
from the Bolshevik Urals Soviet, and Nicholas and his
family were executed.

THE HINDENBURG AND LUDENDORFF FOLLIES

Unrestricted Submarine Warfare
1917 Germany

By William R. Forstchen

The Germans are famously efficient people. When it comes to organizational skills, the marshaling of human resources, the precision of their creations, they are second to none. It's just that when it comes to some of their decision making, their own calculations, which seem so logical at the start, often turn out to be their unmaking. Thus it was with the decision to resume unrestricted submarine warfare in 1917.

The complexities of failed foreign policy that created a two-front war for Germany in 1914 are worthy of a separate essay on folly. Suffice it to say that by 1916, as Germany entered the third year of the Great War, the realization was sinking in that the war would most likely be lost.

By that time Generals Hindenburg and Ludendorff had essentially created a military dictatorship, with the Kaiser serving as little more than a figurehead and rubber stamp for the paragons chosen to guide Germany to victory. For all practical purposes Germany had undergone a military coup in order to stay in the war.

Unfortunately for the Germans the grand plan for a battle of annihilation at Verdun, launched early in 1916, had turned into just that . . . annihilation for both sides rather than just the French. The suicidal British offensive on the Somme was turning into a mutual death pact as well, and since the start of the year the German army had sustained over a million casualties, a loss rate that it could no longer endure. The only bright spot on the ledger was the clear evidence that the czarist armies to the east were tottering toward collapse.

Beyond that, natural resources were becoming an even more crucial problem. With so many young and middle-aged men in the armies, farm production had dropped. Critical war materials such as petroleum products and rubber were all but unavailable due to the stranglehold of the British blockade, and a ration system that was one step removed from outright starvation was imposed.

Against the backdrop of this crisis Hindenburg and Ludendorff struggled to calculate a scientific plan for victory. The evidence was clear that unless Germany could find a winning strategy by 1918, it would be starved and bled out of the fight. The plans of 1916 to militarily and morally shatter the French army had failed. France was on the ropes; in fact it would never again be a significant *offensive* army, but when it came to defending their homeland they were still in the fight. The attempt to challenge the British navy at Jutland had been a tactical victory for the German navy, but a strategic defeat nonetheless since the blockade was still unbroken. Russia looked promising but it seemed that an offensive there would be swallowed up by the vast spaces of the country. Intelligence reports were indicating increasing social unrest and war weariness in Russia, but the team of H and L dismissed this as wishful thinking on the part of their intelligence corps.

Above all else it was the blockade that was strangling the Fatherland and, as the generals considered their alternatives, a counterblockade increasingly seemed like the answer. For a brief period in 1915 Germany had engaged in unrestricted submarine warfare, but the *Luisitania* incident, and the threat of American intervention had ended that.

They cast about for a plan, but any plan to break the deadlock increasingly involved the Imperial Navy in its answer, and the following calculation was offered:

Given X number of German submarines unleashed to engage merchant shipping off the coast of England, it could be reasonably calculated that Y number of ships would be sunk. The crucial number here was the total tonnage of merchant ships available to Great Britain. As a net importer of food and crucial war materials, the dropping of total tonnage below a certain point would result in the breakdown of Britain's war industry and the starvation of its civilians. One could call this point on the graph, the moment when there were no longer enough ships available to supply Britain, Point Z. Therefore, if Y number of ships could be sunk Point Z would be crossed, meaning that Britain could no longer sustain itself.

Here was the race . . . to cross point Z as quickly as possible and hold it there, and then continue to sink ships faster than they could be replaced. It was assumed that Britain would have a small stockpile of reserves, but within several months these would be exhausted. Facing mass starvation, British morale would crack and England would sue for peace. To add weight to the argument Germany would refrain from offensive assaults other than local operations in 1917, with the intent of building up a major strategic reserve, trained in updated tactics, and this new army would launch a smashing blow in the West at the same time that morale in England collapsed.

The one uncertain variable was America. Its industrial capability was already a major factor in the Allied ability to stay in the fight. The two leaders had to assume that, within months of declaring unrestricted warfare, America would enter the fight. Here now was the key part of the mathematical equation. It was calculated that America was so unprepared for war (in 1914 our army was smaller than the forces of Chile, Portugal, or Bulgaria), that it would take a minimum of a year before the first troops could be mobilized, outfitted, trained and shipped over. Once in Europe that army would place an additional strain on dwindling resources as well. H and L's staff calculated that it would take nearly two years before America's armed forces would have any kind of impact, not truly entering the fray until the winter of 1918–19. If the early part of the calculation held up, the war would already be over by then and the Americans would simply turn around and go home.

So that was the calculation. The Z point would be reached within months of the start of the submarine offensive and then held there into 1918. The ground offensive would bring the final pressure to bear. England would crack. France, losing the British support on its left flank, would fold. And victory would be achieved prior to any true American buildup on the Western Front. Full attention could then be turned east and czarist Russia would fold within weeks.

And so the plan was launched on January 31, 1917, with Germany's declaration of a zone of unrestricted submarine warfare around Great Britain. Within weeks several American-flagged ships, some of them originally of British registry but transferred to dummy holding companies in America, were hit. On April 6, 1917, America declared war on Germany. In that same month the plan seemed to be working, with merchantman losses soaring to nearly 900,000 tons. Total available shipping soon drifted down toward the line calculated to bring about starvation. On the Western Front Germany assumed a defensive posture and easily ground up the ill-planned British offensives. Throughout the spring and early summer of 1917 merchant ships were sinking at a rate faster than they could be replaced, and Great Britain's total food reserves dropped to less than a thirty-day supply for the entire nation.

Sixteen months later Germany was on the ropes and mass starvation swept the country, setting the groundwork for the deadliest plague in history, the great influenza epidemic of 1918. The army was in full retreat. So what happened?

What had seemed like sound strategic planning at the time had simply not added up. First was the sustained rate of loses, the Y factor in the calculation. It was assumed that there would be no significant tactical or technological changes on the part of the Allies. The high losses, however, finally triggered the creation of a convoy system, heavily guarded by destroyers and cruisers. The loss rate for the Allies fell, and while not nearly as successful as the Allied antisubmarine campaign would be in 1943, German losses of their precious and difficult-to-manufacture U-boats climbed. The next factor was the

American industrial response. Though poorly organized when compared to 1942, American industrial might was gradually brought to bear and, by late 1917, new systems of ship manufacturing started to make good the losses. By the middle of 1918 American shipbuilders were making replacements faster than they were being sunk. Combined with the convoy system, this meant that the so carefully calculated Z point, though crossed early in the offensive, was not held.

The third and crucial factor was American mobilization. In March 1918, Germany launched its final great offensive in the West. It was a smashing success. The British army, badly battered after the insane offensives of 1916–17, simply cracked under the strain. For a brief period in the spring of 1918 the war on the Western Front became fluid again. German troops drove to within sight of Paris and the French army seemed to be falling apart as well. And then, at Chateau-Thierry, the German army ran smack into American troops. First in the thousands, then the tens of thousands, and by August of 1918 in the hundreds of thousands. Though lacking in experience they more than made up for it with a spirit, an élan, that had not been seen since the opening weeks of the war.

The crowning blow was an unexpected victory elsewhere which helped to lead to defeat . . . and that was the collapse of Russia.

Only four weeks after the beginning of unrestricted submarine warfare, an anticzarist coup erupted in Petrograd, and within two weeks Czar Nicholas II abdicated. Several advisors to Hindenburg and Ludendorff begged for reconsideration of the master plan. There was still time to call off the unrestricted warfare in the Atlantic and, if need be, to make amends to the Americans, thus keeping them out of the fight. All attention, instead, should now be put on Russia, which was disintegrating into chaos and revolution. Push here, the advisors cried, and within the year Russia would be out of the fight. Once this was accomplished the vast resources of the steppes would more than make good any problems created by the Allied blockade. Then the army could be pulled out of Russia and, newly invigorated by victory in the East, the battle could be pressed to victory in the West.

It would have worked. But Hindenburg and Ludendorff saw Russia as a quagmire and had no desire to throw German troops into that front, though they did make one key decision about Lenin that is the topic of another essay. So here is the oddest part of all. The submarine plan was pushed and Russia collapsed anyhow. Rather than ease up on the stretched demands of German manpower it made it worse because Germany was finally forced to pull nearly a million men out of its strategic reserves to occupy the Ukraine and other territories ceded by the Treaty of Brest-Litovsk, which took Russia out of the fight in March 1918.

Thus did victory in the East, unexpected and unaccounted for, drain off a million men from the 1918 offensive, which now had to be launched as a desperate gamble, not as a follow-up on on exhausted foe in the West but rather in a bid to forestall the growing American commitment.

In the Argonne Forest in September 1918, over a million American troops, provoked into a fight, and contrary to all predictions, came on with a vengeance. The German army, now overextended, cracked apart and started the retreat that would lead to the armistice.

JUST TO MAKE TROUBLE

Germany Smuggles Lenin Into Russia
1917 Europe

William R. Forstchen

For three long years he had been trapped in Switzerland, as much a prisoner of war as the hundreds of thousands of Russian troops languishing in German, Austrian, and Turkish prison camps. Exiled from Russia prior to the start of World War I, Vladimir Ilyich Lenin had found a safe refuge in Switzerland where he continued to coordinate the underground activities of his small Bolshevik Party.

With the onset of hostilities, however, his tenuous links back to Russia grew increasingly fragile. The governments of France and Italy, to the west and south of Switzerland, had arrest warrants waiting for Lenin as an enemy of the Allied cause if he should dare to try and set foot across the border. As a citizen of an enemy nation he would be arrested as well if he headed north or east, into Germany or the Austrian Empire. Contact was reduced to occasional courier messages and coded tele-

grams. So he was stuck, seething with frustration as the
hated czarist government collapsed in March 1917 and
was replaced with a republic headed by Alexander Kerensky. Lenin felt trapped by his circumstances, unable to
participate in the opportunity he had plotted more than
thirty years for, the establishment of a communist state
in Russia.

He briefly considered donning a disguise, attempting
a crossing of France with forged papers, and trying to
take a boat to Russia from there. An absurd plan since it
was assumed that Allied intelligence agents were keeping
a close watch on him.

Finally he struck on a plan that had a certain surreal
quality to it . . . he would approach the Germans for help.
Meeting with the German minister in Bern, Lenin laid out
his proposal . . . that Germany would provide transport
across their country and help to smuggle him into Finland. From there he would go into Russia, raise a revolution, seize control of the government, and then pull Russia
out of the war, thereby freeing Germany to turn its full
power to the Western Front.

The German minister in Bern, along with his intelligence advisors, must have had a difficult time concealing
his grin of amusement over this mad, wild-eyed scheme.
It was estimated that the Bolsheviks numbered less than
50,000 throughout all of Russia. Granted, they had created
problems for the Kerensky government's war effort, but
the thought of a communist takeover was as insane as
Lenin's proclamation that Germany would fall to communism as well. Nevertheless the decision was made to approve it. At the very least it would provide a bit of
consternation for the Western Allies, who were terrified
that Russia might bail out of the war and it might even

help to trigger further revolts in the Russian army, which was already disintegrating in the confusion resulting from the overthrow of the czar. Lenin and eighteen others were thus sealed into a railroad car, transported across Germany in secret, and then shipped over to Finland. The German minister in Bern, and the military advisors who had approved the project, assumed that this would be the last ever heard of Lenin. Even if he caused a brief disruption, he'd be dead within a month. That in itself wouldn't have been bad either. At least he wouldn't be around to create problems after Germany won the war. But, as Winston Churchill later reflected, Germany had "turned upon Russia the most grisly of all weapons. They transported Lenin in a seal truck like a plague bacillus from Switzerland into Russia."

"Never wish too hard for something, you just might get it," was what more than one German official on the Eastern Front and government representative in Moscow felt a year and a half later. Lenin had indeed pulled it off. When Germany had first presented the bill after the successful coup, with its harsh demands for territorial concessions, including all of the Ukraine, Lenin balked. Finally, the German government was forced to divert forces from the pending offensive on the Western Front to back up their demands, and they renewed operations on the Russian Front in February 1918. A month later Lenin agreed to the Treaty of Brest-Litovsk. The problem, though, was that Germany was now forced to occupy its new territories. Hundreds of thousands of troops disappeared into the east as occupation troops on a little-understood campaign that would take some of them all the way to the Caspian Sea.

By the early summer of 1918 the German government viewed the monster it had created in the east with increasing concern. Though there was allegedly a peace on the Eastern Front, independent Soviets in the occupied territories were talking openly about the pending global revolution and, more shockingly, of Germany as the next target. Increasingly, German troops were getting involved in the secret support of counterrevolutionary White units, a most ironic mix since the Allies were supporting the Whites as well. Trotsky, head of the Red Army, also spoke of the need to liberate the rest of Eastern Europe, and declared that the liberation of Germany was an obligation to their prophet, Marx. Back on the home front, underground communist cells in Germany were looking to Russia for support. In a wild last-minute reversal, the German government now considered a plan to somehow kidnap the czar from the Bolsheviks and put him back on the throne. Before the operation could be launched Kaiser Wilhelm's unfortunate cousin, along with the rest of his family, were murdered at Lenin's order. Shortly thereafter the war collapsed on the Germans, and they signed an armistice with the West, an armistice that would lead a year later to the brutal terms imposed at Versailles.

The greatest terror now was not the Western Allies, but rather the specter of a communist revolution imported from Russia. With the signing of the armistice, any attempt to hold the Ukraine, the Baltic states, and what would be the new state of Poland collapsed as well. Throughout the 1920s the majority of citizens in Germany lived in dread of what Lenin had created. Many finally came to think that a strong shield held by an iron fist was their only hope. A disgruntled former corporal, who saw the sealed railroad car as part of the knife in the back of the German war effort, found that this fear of Bolshevism was an excellent tool for recruiting new members to his own political cause, Nazism.

Germany gained nothing, and for the rest of the century most of the world paid a high price for what they unleashed. Without their decision there would likely have been no Communist revolution, probably no Nazi Party, and no Cold War to bankrupt half the globe. As for the minister in Bern, and the intelligence officers in Switzerland and Berlin who had approved the scheme to send Lenin back to Russia . . . well, all that could be said was that, at the time, they thought they were doing the right thing.

STRANGLE THE MONSTER
IN THE CRADLE

But Make Sure You Do It Right
1917–22 Russia

by William R. Forstchen

The Bolshevik takeover had caught everyone by surprise. The Western Allies, France, Britain, and America, had assumed that Lenin and his people would attempt some sort of trouble. They had repeatedly warned the Kerensky government which had overthrown the czar back in March to be on the lookout, or better yet simply to track Lenin down and assassinate him, but they had never really expected that Lenin would not only stage a coup but actually succeed in taking Petrograd and Moscow.

For the Allies, it was an unmitigated disaster. Russia had been the bloody foil that had absorbed millions of German, Austrian and Turkish troops during four years of war. To prop up the czar a massive effort was launched to ship supplies in via Murmansk and across the Pacific to the eastern shore of Siberia. After the czar fell, more supplies had been promised to keep Kerensky in the fight, and in the summer of 1917 the three major Allies had even started to position troops at the supply heads to protect the equipment and also to serve as a base of support for Kerensky. When Lenin signed Russia out of the war he promptly ordered all Allied troops off Russian soil . . . and the new war was on.

It's a little-known aspect of the relationship between the West and the Soviets, the years 1917–22. For all practical purposes it was a war, and we fought and lost.

There were several conflicting reasons why the Allies should get involved in Russia at a time when Britain, certainly, and France, more so, were desperately fighting for their lives on the Western Front. The most pragmatic and straightforward view was that hundreds of millions of dollars of military hardware had been shipped into Russia. With Russia now out of the war that equipment should be returned immediately, and our troops were there to insure the return. The more venturesome added that Lenin's hold on power was tenuous at best. Various proczarists, pro-Kerenskyites, military warlords, and nationalistic groups such as the Ukrainians and Lithuanians, were all dead set against Lenin; and should be supported in the cynical long-term hope of luring Russia back into the fight against Germany. Finally there were a few men, such as Winston Churchill, who had the foresight to realize that if the communists were ever allowed to set down roots in Russia the whole world might one day be threatened by an amoral, murderous regime. Churchill openly declared that the "red monster" should be killed in the cradle before it was allowed to grow.

So the Western Allies decided to intervene. It was a remarkably good idea, one that with a little planning, foresight, and willingness to make a commitment, might very well have finished off Lenin by 1919. And it was bungled from beginning to end.

Tens of thousands of British, French and American troops arrived via Murmansk, through the Middle East, and across the Pacific, and none of them had any clear rules of engagement or clear policy other than to hold onto the supply stockpiles. Meanwhile Trotsky, commander of the Red Army, turned from front to front in a brilliant series of campaigns, repelling repeated drives to take Moscow, while at the same time expanding operations eastward over the Urals, linking up isolated posts along the trans-Siberian railroad, and fomenting rebellion against the Germans and Western forces in the Ukraine.

To make matters worse, the Allies themselves served as a damning bit of propaganda for the xenophobic Russians. Lenin was able to declare that the Allies had simply used Russians as bodies to absorb German bullets while they grew rich and advanced their own cause (not entirely untrue), that foreign invaders and their mercenary hirelings were now tromping about on Russian soil (an argument the Americans had used effectively in 1776), and that the Reds were the only true force for the salvation of Russia.

After November 1918 and the signing of the armistice, the primary political reason for keeping the various expeditionary forces in Russia was lost. Germany had lost, and part of the agreement was that it had to return its forces back to within its 1914 borders, thus ending the occupation of the Ukraine. Churchill, who was essentially out of power at this point, and a few others now argued even more loudly that, with the pressure off in the west, troops could be sent straight into Russia via the Baltic states and the Black Sea. Now was the chance to kill off the murderous Reds. Every one of their statements was used by Le-

nin's propaganda machine to stoke up nationalistic fervor
and convince political moderates and socialists who were
not communists to ally under his banner. Lenin's appeal
worked, while Churchill's fell on deaf ears.

Meanwhile, in the Ukraine, there were cases of British-
and French-supported White units linking up with retreating German units, who were fighting at times for simple survival, or actually hiring out as mercenaries. This
only confused the matter even further. Poles, Ukrainians,
and Lithuanians banded together briefly to form an anticommunist coalition but then, as was typical of the region,
had a falling out between themselves, and the Ukraine
was soon back in the Leninist fold. One hundred thousand anticommunist Czech prisoners of war had been
freed by the Kerensky government with the understanding that they could return to the west and there serve as
a liberation force for a free Czechoslovakia, but the Reds
backed off from the promise. So this hundred-thousand-
man army, trapped in Siberia, seized arms stockpiles and
took over most of the trans-Siberian railroad. They even
came close to liberating the czar before he was executed.
The Czechs now turned east, moving toward Vladivostok.
Linking up with the American expeditionary force in that
region they stayed on, creating widespread trouble until
finally shipping out through an agreement with the
Americans. This modern anabasis finally ended back in
the new republic of Czechoslovakia after a voyage circling
the globe. Ironically some of these same men were forced
back into the army when the Nazis took over in 1939,
wound up back in Russia and again became prisoners
in 1945.

Ultimately the entire affair had an ignominious end.
As soon as the war was over the western governments,

showing their usual lack of forethought, and succumbing to the war weariness gripping the world, ordered their units out. The last ones pulled out in 1920, though Japanese units, hoping to take advantage of the general anarchy and hold on to part of Siberia, stayed until 1922. At one point the tension between the Japanese and American garrisons in Russia almost broke out into armed conflict, a foreshadowing of things to come.

Without any direction the plan to split Russia between Red and White governments had been worst than useless. It gave Lenin much-needed fodder for his propaganda, dragged out a bitter war, and helped to stoke generations of anti-Western propaganda. Even into the 1980s Western tourists, this writer included, were reminded that America had once invaded Russia.

Given the seventy years of rule that followed and the uneasy peace which exists at this very moment, Churchill was right. The monster should have been strangled in the cradle. The half-hearted effort, instead, only helped it to grow and devour millions.

REILLY BUSTS "THE TRUST"

Soviet Shadow Organization Exposed
1926 Moscow

By Brian M. Thomsen

After the successful Leninist Russian Revolution of 1917, the new Soviet governing bodies had to be on their guard against various counterrevolutionary interests, as well as foreign governments looking to subvert their fledgling republic.

Felix Dzerzhinsky was appointed to head up an organization whose title explained its goal—the All-Russian Extraordinary Commission for Combating Counterrevolution and Sabotage. The organization's title was shortened to just "the Cheka" and it was the forerunner of what was eventually the KGB.

Dzerzhinsky realized that the best way to keep tabs on the enemies of the republic was by having observers (spies) in their midst. He furthered his intelligence-gathering goals by actually helping to set up a group whose announced intention was the overthrow of the Soviet regime. Such a group would obviously attract members of

any underground resistance working within Russia or
abroad, thus making their identities known to the Cheka.
This group was called "the Trust."

"The Trust" was made up of Soviet emigres who desired to overthrow the communists and reestablish the
rule of the White Russians. Most of its members were
societal dilettantes who waxed poetic about the old days
of the Romanovs and were more than willing to raise
money for various resistance groups supposedly working
within the Soviet Union. Substantial financial aid was also
solicited and obtained by "the Trust" from both the
United States and British governments.

Using this front organization, Dzerzhinsky was able
to control outside propaganda against the Soviet Union,
as well as lure various enemies of the state back within
Soviet borders so that they could be imprisoned, interro-
gated, and executed quietly.

"The Trust" was the magnum opus of the Soviet intelligence community until direct orders from Stalin himself
led it to instigate an action that exposed its true nature to
its enemies.

Sidney Reilly had been a thorn in the side of communist Russia since before the Cheka even existed. The son
of an Irish sea captain and a Russian Jewish mother, Reilly
was one of British intelligence's first freelance agents. In
addition to numerous pre-World War I accomplishments,
he is largely considered to be the chief engineer of the
Lettish plot during the Russian Revolution, in which the
troops from Lett and Latvia who acted as bodyguards for
the chief Bolsheviks were to seize Lenin and Trotsky, and
thus allow Reilly and his associates to take control of the
government. The plot failed when one of the Lett agents
seized an opportunity to attempt an assassination of Lenin

(which failed) and tipped Reilly's hand to the opposition, forcing Reilly to flee Russia with a price on his head.

On returning to Britain, Reilly attempted to warn both British and American intelligence concerns of the insidiousness of the Bolshevik regime, and is believed to have tried to raise financing to reenter Russia and attempt another revolution from within. Reilly was equally suspicious of the various White Russian organizations which he considered, for the most part, to be ineffective and dangerous to the cause, and he knew that the Bolshevik machine had infiltrated all of their organizations, and was managing somehow to always remain a full step ahead of all resistance efforts.

When "the Trust," as directed by the Cheka, approached Reilly to help him enter the country through Finland, he became suspicious, and set up a fail-safe mechanism to alert his various British contacts that if anything happened to him, obviously "the Trust" was to blame, and was therefore not to be trusted.

Reilly entered Russia via Finland as planned and was instantly arrested by the Cheka. Dzerzhinsky shrewdly realized the trap that he had fallen into, and started to initiate a plan whereby Reilly would be rescued by agents of "the Trust" and returned to England, but this plan was vetoed by his superior, Stalin, who had no desire to see one of the great enemies of the Soviet Republic slip out of their hands. Sources also indicate that Stalin had begun to take notice of the influence that Dzerzhinsky was exerting and felt that the dissolution of "the Trust" would help undercut any power base that might later threaten his own.

Though the details of Reilly's fate remain uncertain to this day, it is assumed that he was executed within a year of his arrest upon entering Russia. The British Secret Service, of course, denied any affiliation with his mission, and do to this day. They did, however, spread the rumors as to the suspect loyalty of "the Trust," and that organization was widely discredited and eventually ceased to exist.

Dzerzhinsky's masterwork had succeeded in capturing the man who was probably the greatest threat to its existence, but in doing so, had laid itself bare to public scrutiny. When he died in 1926, the Cheka had grown in strength from 15,000 to 250,000. Part of this group was needed to suppress dissent at home, but the majority had its attention turned toward Britain whose Reilly-led conspiracies still gave them cause to fear . . . and at this juncture they had yet to establish their own double agents within the ranks of the enemy.

How to Train an Enemy

Russia and Germany Cut a Deal
1930s Russia

by William R. Forstchen

The development of German armor is a classic case study of the good idea that comes back to bite you later. Their vaunted methodic planning certainly led to ghastly repercussions.

Many people think that it was Germany that had always been on the cutting edge of armor development, an absolutely groundless assumption. In fact it was the British who opened the field. As early as 1915 a small band of English visionaries, encouraged by a young Winston Churchill, were already advocating the idea that the "tank" (a cover code name for the development of this new weapon) could be the weapon to break the stalemate on the Western Front. Production started on several models, the great mistake being that higher command decided to throw each new weapon in as it was produced rather than all in one massive surprise attack. Primitive as the machines were, and in spite of the tactical ineptness of their first deployments, the weapon showed great promise.

Early in 1918 a study group was put together under a young British officer named J. F. C. Fuller, and given the task of planning a breakthrough offensive that could win the war by 1919. Fuller's final draft of Plan 1919 called for some remarkable high-tech weapons and applications. The grand offensive would be initiated by heavy long-range bombers attacking far behind the lines, taking out transportation, communications, and command centers. This attack would be augmented by troops who would leap from planes and use parachutes to land, and sow further confusion.

Meanwhile, at the main front, twin columns made up of tanks, armored personnel carriers, ammunition carriers and self-propelled artillery would smash through the front after a short, intensive barrage. The columns, spaced fifty miles apart, would charge deep into the enemy lines and punch through to the rear, bypassing any strong points. Riding with the column would be radio operators who would stay in touch with hundreds of bomber planes circling overhead, calling them in to strafe, bomb and smash down any resistance. The columns would finally pivot toward each other and link up, cutting off a couple of thousand square miles and leaving a hole in the German lines fifty miles wide for the infantry to pour through.

Sounds familiar? Fuller never got a chance to try out his grand plan; the Germans collapsed and an armistice was signed six months before his offensive was to be attempted. Fuller's plans were set aside because final victory had been achieved by mass firepower and heavy infantry assaults. Within several years he was begging for just a couple of dozen surplus tanks for training back in England. His plans, however, were published and studied intensely by the former foes who were to be the recipients of the attack.

For the Germans, Fuller's plan offered a quick, stunning, fairly inexpensive and low-manpower path to victory in a future conflict. This is one aspect of armored warfare that is often overlooked as an impetus for the Germans; it allowed short, swift conflicts without mass mobilization or high casualties. But the Versailles Treaty of 1919 strictly forbade any armor beyond a few armored cars useful only for crowd control, all artillery beyond a few light-caliber pieces, any offensive aircraft and any type of maneuvers or war games as well.

So the problem became how to figure it all out and test this wild new theory. Secretly, board games were held to test it, but any type of field exercise would have required hundreds of square miles of territory and thousands of men. It would be impossible to peform such a maneuver without the Allies getting wind of it and shutting the entire program down. The top command of the Weimar Republic's army cast about for a solution. It was realized that someday the Versailles restrictions would finally be dropped, but if they didn't get their planning in now, and test this new idea out, Germany would be so far behind that it would be impossible to ever catch up, let alone leap ahead in arms development.

Finally a rather strange notion was put forward. The only other pariah in Europe was the Soviet Union. Undoubtedly the Soviets were playing around with armor theory, so why not throw in with them? Out in the vast steppes of Russia there were hundreds of thousands of square miles of ground to play on, far from the prying eyes of any Western observer. Theories could be tested, maneuvers conducted using the vast manpower of the Red Army, and no one would be the wiser. It would be easy to arrange for German expertise and theory to be exchanged for the use of Russian resources and personnel (German forces also having been curtailed). A few conservative heads were stunned by the suggestion. The Reds were a loose cannon. Only a couple of years before they had almost taken out Poland in a brief and bloody war. Why give them the foundation for a whole new theory of warfare? The response was dismissive, the Russians were primitive, their industry still at a nineteenth century level, they would never be able to use these tools on their own.

And so a secret deal was struck between the Red Army and the Weimar army, to conduct joint research and maneuvers in central Russia to study armored theory. Within months a select team of German theoreticians was deep inside Soviet Russia, where they hooked up with their counterparts in the Red Army. Special units of the Red Army were detailed to serve as opposing armies. Trucks were used to simulate tanks, armored personnel carriers, self-propelled guns, and mobile command centers. The few planes then available to the Red Army buzzed about overhead.

For several summers the war games were held, each game building on the last. Techniques for initial breakthroughs were developed, along with innovations in the use of mobile command and control centers, headquarters on wheels outfitted with the latest high-tech radio equipment so that a commander could stay in touch with his far-flung columns and air support overhead. Infantry support tactics were developed as well, with the thought that infantry should ride directly into battle with the tanks and dismount when needed to mop up dangerous strong points and antitank positions. How to blunt such attacks was studied as well, with close attention paid to the ideas of defense in depth, interlocking antitank defenses, and the need for mobile reaction forces.

And so, throughout the late twenties and into the early thirties, German and Red Army officers exchanged views, worked together in the field, and even built friendships based on their mutual interests in this new high-tech warfare.

With the Nazi rise to power and its emphasis on racial superiority and anticommunism, this exchange program finally collapsed. By 1936 there was no longer a need for it anyhow. The Treaty of Versailles had been renounced and Germany could now freely conduct maneuvers on its own territory. The wealth of information gleaned from the Russian studies was put to good use as German industry geared up to produce weapons specified by the experiments out on the steppes . . . light mobile tanks for rapid advance, heavy mainline tanks for follow-up punch, tracked personnel carriers for infantry support and as ammunition and weapons carriers, mobile 88mm guns which could quickly be moved for support, and the deadly Stuka divebomber for pinpoint attacks against enemy strong points.

This force tore across Poland in less than two weeks. The following spring it annihilated the French and British armies in a brilliant six-week campaign that captured the Low Countries and France while sustaining just a minor fraction of the casualties taken from 1914–18.

Then came the invasion of Russia. Hitler's planners declared that Russia would be a six-week war. Thanks to the Soviets' forward deployment of troops and inadequate armor, the war would be one of massive envelopment along the frontier. Once the Red Army was destroyed, Leningrad, Moscow, and the industrial heartland of the Ukraine would fall. By winter the line of occupation was expected to stretch from Astrakhan in the south to Murmansk in the north.

For the first couple of months all seemed to be going as planned. One after another Soviet divisions, corps, and entire armies were scratched off the list maintained by the German high command. By early August, on paper at least, the Red Army had ceased to exist. But that didn't seem to be true in the field, as new divisions by the dozens, and finally the hundreds, were thrown into the fight. The true shock, however, was the armor. Rather than antiquated third-rate machines, the Germans started to run into a new, unimagined medium-weight tank . . . the now legendary T-34. Its turret was welded together and presented sloping armor. Its 75mm gun could outpunch anything the Germans had, and perhaps worst of all its wide treads could traverse snow, mud, and swampy ground with ease while the narrower treads of German tanks, designed for warfare in western Europe, sank into the quagmire.

By December thousands of these machines were swarming the German lines, tearing apart German tanks with ease, slashing massive holes in the frozen German lines, and triggering a panic-stricken retreat. Where the hell had this nightmare come from?

The seedling planted by the joint war games of the 1920s and early 30s had borne fruit with the Soviets as well. The difference was that while the Germans paraded their new weapons around at the latest party rallies, the Soviets had kept their armor program hidden; with factories, training fields, and entire divisional formations concealed far out in the steppes of central Russia. The early maneuvers and war games had trained the new generation of Soviet tank experts. Though still lacking in the high-tech communications gear, and deciding to concentrate everything on tanks rather than armored personnel carriers and self-propelled guns (the infantry simply rode in atop the tanks, and the 75mm gun on the T-34 served as artillery support), the lessons of the German maneuvers were now being put to good use. That wacky notion of the German high command was now going down in defeat, since without truly realizing it, they had managed to train their future enemies as well.

CHOOSE YOUR ALLIES CAREFULLY

Or Sometimes Your Best Friends Can Be Your Worst Enemies 1939 Germany and Italy

by William R. Forstchen

In the beginning the relationship had been that of mentor and student. The first fascist takeover in post-World War I Europe had been the Black Shirt rebellion in Italy, and Benito Mussolini, a former newspaper reporter and political hack who staged a march on Rome in 1922, was granted virtual dictatorial powers by the parliament and king in November of that year. It was shortly thereafter that a rabble rouser in Munich, citing Mussolini as his example, attempted a coup, his headquarters a beer hall, and was thrown in jail.

Ten years later that same dissident took power in Germany and immediately turned to Mussolini for friendship and guidance. Politically it was an interesting move for Austria and Germany, who had been traditional rivals against Italy. This was certainly true when in the First War, Italy had bailed out of an alliance with Austria and Germany as the conflict started, and a year later came in on the side of the Allies. But in the name of fascist solidarity the past was forgotten. An alliance was soon formed, the famed Axis Pact, so named by Mussolini as an axis of power joining Rome to Berlin.

Having Mussolini as an ally, however, was like having an overlarge, boisterous and loud-mouthed brother-in-law whom one constantly has to bail out of jail and financial difficulties. Throughout the 20s and early 30s Mussolini had pumped up the idea of a return to Roman greatness, that the Mediterranean was destined to again be an Italian lake. After suppressing rebellion in Libya, Mussolini turned his eyes toward Ethiopia. Ethiopia was the only nation in all of Africa which had successfully resisted European imperialism. It was therefore essential to Italian nationalistic pride that this be forgotten and Mussolini set off on a murderous adventure, employing airpower and poison gas against troops armed with single shot rifles.

Though Hitler was forced to publicly applaud the heroic actions of his Italian ally, secretly he was distressed. Why anyone would want Ethiopia in the first place was beyond him, and Mussolini's actions served as a warning notice about fascism at the time, as did Mussolini's blunders while defeating the Ethiopians.

As Hitler moved toward his own aggressive actions, Mussolini urged him on and gradually the roles reversed, with Hitler as the dominant power and Mussolini as the somewhat amusing sidekick. Mussolini almost triggered another crisis in April 1939 when he preemptively seized Albania, thereby saddling Italy with a responsibility to that troubled nation which it regrets to this day. This seizure tightened the relationship between Greece and Britain and served as well to increase tensions throughout the

Balkans. Though Romania and Bulgaria had fallen into the fascist orbit, Yugoslavia still had to be reckoned with.

When war began in 1939 between Germany, France and England, Hitler turned to his favorite ally and suggested that it would be a good idea for Mussolini to join in, and thus pin down crucial British and French assets in the Mediterranean. Mussolini's slippery nature really came to the fore when, after all his bluster and posturing, he flatly refused. It was, in fact, a smart decision on his part, at least as far as Italian destiny went, for the prospect of facing the combined British and French Mediterranean fleets was not a positive one. Mussolini sat out the first nine months of the war until Germany had already defeated France, when Mussolini saw a chance to grab up a slice from his border with that country. His cowardly backstab of France in the last days of the campaign drew derisive comments from the entire world, even including Hitler.

Italy now prepared its forces in Libya . . . the goal, the fulfillment of the Italian dream of the Mediterranean as a Roman lake. In September 1940 the Italian army launched itself against the British forces in Egypt with the goal of seizing the Suez Canal. In terms of the overall German strategic plan, the taking of the Suez might be helpful eventually, but at that particular moment it was hoped that England would be out of the fight before much longer. In the German opinion, the Italians were only serving to tie down some overseas troops, at best. For the Italians it was a debacle.

The British army, in a brilliant counterstrike, tore around the Italian army, struck into the rear and destroyed a force four times bigger than itself. At the same time another British force struck in the opposite direction, taking out the Italian colonies of Ethiopia and Somaliland, the first fascist territories liberated in World War II. It was a tremendous blow to Italian prestige.

There was yet another Italian offensive now underway, a strike out of Albania into Greece. It was a move Hitler had expressly told Mussolini not to attempt. He had created a long-term fascist plan for the rest of the Balkans, but now was not the time to overextend. Invading Greece might only result in a British lodgment in the Balkans as a response. Mussolini went ahead anyhow, attacked, and was not only stopped but, by the following spring, his army was in a headlong dash back into Albania with a combined Greek and British army in hot pursuit.

It could not have come at a worse time. Throughout the winter Hitler had turned his attention eastward with the decision to invade Russia as soon as the spring thaw was over, with a planned kickoff of the offensive for the middle of May 1941. As a student of military history he well remembered the last great invasion of Russia, by Napoleon, which had not been launched until the last week in June. Napoleon had reached Moscow by September but had not been able to consolidate his position before the onset of autumn, and thus lost everything. A May offensive would put his forces in Moscow by mid to late summer, with plenty of time to wrap up operations before the winter snows.

Now the situation in the Balkans threatened that timetable. If Italy was kicked out of Albania, Yugoslavia could very well fall firmly into the British camp. British positions in Greece could threaten Romania and Bulgaria as well, perhaps even posing a threat to the vital Ploesti oil fields, which were the sole major source of oil for the Nazi war machine.

Hitler was left with few options. First he was forced to dispatch a brilliant up-and-coming panzer general, Erwin Rommel, into Africa to try to turn around the situation in Libya. As for Albania and Greece there seemed to be only one alternative left. Putting Barbarossa, the invasion of Russia, on hold, Hitler swung an entire army around and catapulted it into Yugoslavia on April 6, 1941. The campaign was a brilliant feat of German weaponry. Losing less than a thousand men the Germans inflicted upwards of 100,000 casualties on the Yugoslavians. Another German army slashed into Greece, topping the operation with the famed airborne assault on Crete in May. In less than two months, for losses of less than ten thousand men, the Germans had achieved what was impossible for Italy; the capture of Greece, the destruction of British forces occupying the region, and the supposed capture of Yugoslavia.

But ultimately the Italian debacle in Libya started a gradual trickle of Germans into a theater of operations where they had not meant to be . . . North Africa. By 1942 Germany had diverted well over a hundred thousand men to this region, a hundred thousand who might have made a crucial difference around Stalingrad. Barbarossa had finally been launched, but six weeks later than originally planned, due to the diversion into the Balkans. Further delayed by a bitter-freeze, Hitler's armies advanced six months later to within sight of the Kremlin and then were driven back in the first week of December. By early 1943 nearly 300,000 Germans were committed to supporting efforts in North Africa, and nearly all of them were lost. With that defeat North Africa would serve as a springboard for still further bloody combat in Italy and on into the south of France.

Perhaps the bloodiest commitment of all, though, was in Yugoslavia. Initially suppressed and thought to be secured, the Germans withdrew nearly all their troops from the region, leaving the occupation to the Italians. Of course Mussolini bungled the operation. By 1942 the situation had begun to turn as various resistance groups, the key one being Tito's communist partisans, organized and began to strike back. By 1943 Yugoslavia was a bleeding wound, a place of implacable and bitter fighting between communist partisans, royalists, nationalists, Italians, and Germans. Vast areas of Yugoslavia were liberated and at one point a full-size airfield was opened by Tito to receive regular flights of supplies sent over from Allied-occupied Italy, the only one of its kind inside occupied Europe. Germany was finally forced to commit an entire army to the region and, like the guerilla combat in Spain during the Napoleonic War, Yugoslavia became one of the most dreaded assignments for a German soldier. It was a war with no quarter. Hitler's astonishingly masterful plan was one of many fateful decisions upon which the outcome of World War II depended.

As for the smart move of allying with Mussolini, Il Duce tried to pay Hitler back by sending an Italian army of nearly two hundred thousand men into Russia. It was a little-known campaign, this Italian expedition across the steppes, and it was on this front that the Italians suffered more battle deaths than on any other front in World War II. The Italian army was assigned the task of guarding the flank of the German Sixth Army, locked in the bitter struggle at Stalingrad. And it was against this hapless army that the Russians threw their massive weight for the breakthrough and encirclement of that city. The Italians crumbled under the blow and were annihilated, leaving the way open for the destruction of the Sixth Army.

Yet Hitler stayed loyal to his old mentor right to the end. When the Allies invaded Italy in 1943, the king of Italy, a shadowy figure in the history of that period, banded together with the parliament and actually ordered Mussolini from office. Surprisingly he went without a fight, was arrested and Italy declared itself out of the war. Hitler sent a top commando squad to rescue Mussolini from house arrest, sent him to the north of his country, which was still behind Axis lines, and set him up in a puppet government.

When the end came in 1945 Mussolini tried to flee the country, but was cornered by Italian partisans, shot, dragged through the streets, and hung upside down from a gas station sign. Even in death Mussolini influenced Hitler. There had been some effort within the Führer's bunker to convince Hitler to try for a breakout from the besieging Russians. Somehow a photograph of Mussolini, hanging inverted alongside his mistress, made it down into the bunker and Hitler, stunned by the photo, passed it around, declaring that never would he run the risk of such an ignominious end. Shortly thereafter he retired to his private quarters and put a bullet through his head.

Given his track record, it's lucky for the Allies that Mussolini had not decided to throw in on our side instead.

BUILD A FORT, BUT LEAVE THE BACK DOOR OPEN

The Maginot Line
1939 France

By William R. Forstchen

Consider the Battle of Camerone, where sixty French foreign legionnaires got themselves snared in a trap and were overwhelmed by three thousand Mexicans during the French invasion of Mexico in the 1860s. Camerone is now celebrated as the high holy day of the legion, complete with the ritualistic parading of the wooden hand of the commander of the doomed unit. So it is with the Maginot Line. To this day French military historians argue that the line was actually the perfect scheme, a glorious effort to minimize the effects of war, which only failed because the Germans and the useless allies, Belgium and Great Britain, failed to do their part. It was, to the French, the ultimate plan, but there certainly seems to be a perverse side to the French.

From 1914–16 the French army was motivated by one sole philosophy, this principle, finding its origins in Napoleonic tactics, declared that regardless of technological advances, an army imbued with a fanatic spirit to attack would always overwhelm its opponent. The cost of this, in the face of machine guns and rapid-fire artillery, was approximately a million dead by 1916, nearly half of them at Verdun alone. By the end of that year the French army broke down in mutiny. The French high command did agree to suspend offensive operations, and struggled to regain control of the army.

In 1918 France did resume limited offensive operations, with the greatest of caution. But after the close of the war, French thinking, arrested by the horrific losses in the trenches, shifted entirely to a defensive philosophy. For the previous three centuries, ever since the brilliant career of the engineer Vauban under Louis XIV, France had been acknowledged as the preeminent master of military engineering. The fortifications around Verdun, though antiquated and poorly manned, had blunted the worst of the German offensive in that region. So, while German, Russian, American and British staffs started weighing various offensive systems to break the gridlock of the trenches, the French formulated the Maginot Line named after a French government minister who pushed the program.

Tentative construction started in the late twenties and by the early thirties, in spite of the global economic crisis, construction went into high gear. It was, with one exception (to be discussed in another essay) the most extensive attempt at fortifications in the history of the world. Hundreds of millions of tons of concrete were poured along a line that stretched from the Swiss border to just south of the Ardennes, at the junction of the borders of France, Luxembourg and Belgium.

It truly was a remarkable feat of engineering, often

more than 100 feet deep, with barracks, theaters, hospitals, and a narrow-guage railroad. Since it was assumed that poison gas would be used in the next war, including some of the dreadful new nerve toxins, elaborate air-filtration systems were intalled, complete with positive-pressure systems and high-tech air locks. Given the need to maintain morale for an army still shaken by its experience in the last war, every convenience was thought of. The best wines, chefs, even art, were provided in quantity. These were just the conveniences.

Topside the line was studded with weapons. Heavy artillery pieces were completely concealed underground. When ready to fire massive hydraulic systems would pull back a camouflaged steel cupola, the piece would rise up, fire, then disappear back under the earth. Lighter field-pieces were set in heavily reinforced concrete and steel bastions. Machine-gun positions covered all approaches, some of the weapons situated so that they could be fired automatically by troops who sat protected underground and guided the weapon with periscopes. Millions of mines, contact, timer set, and remote-controlled, covered all approaches, as did hundreds of thousands of miles of barbwire entanglements. In the event of war, or a crisis, the standing garrisons would be reinforced by reserve formations rushed up from the interior. The fortress line could then be sealed off, ready to face any attack the Germans might be insane enough to throw their way.

There was only one problem . . . in their infinite wisdom the French left the back door open, or more precisely, their entire left flank.

The origin of this was diplomatic. When first designed the Maginot Line was to run from the Swiss border to the Channel, over four hundred miles. And then the question of Belgium intervened. Belgium had been a loyal ally in the First World War, but now had declared itself to be firmly committed to neutrality. So firm was this commitment that the Belgians made it clear that they viewed an extension of the Maginot Line along their border, a flat open section stretching well over a hundred and fifty miles from the Ardennes to the sea, as a "defensively offensive" act. In other words, building the line would mean that the French were ignoring their neutrality and therefore Belgium would be forced to seek its own solution with Germany. The French countered with the proposal that Belgium and Luxembourg coordinate the development of a grand defensive line, working together. No, this was impossible, came the reply, for to do so would violate neutrality and serve as a provocation to Germany.

It's an understatement to declare that the Belgian policy stands as one of the supreme models of narrow-minded folly. But the French, for their part, made some pretty stupid moves next. The French response . . . they stopped building the line north of the Ardennes and waited. They did not even make a half-hearted effort at fortifying key strategic points to the north, such as crossings of the Meuse or major rail and road junctions, such as Amiens. The defenses were only half built . . . it was the equivalent of building a dam halfway across a river and then expecting the river to stop. Part of the later argument regarding this policy was that the financial strain of building the first half of the line had drained France's resources, although they should have saved extra for this, since it was the northern plains that had been the traditional route of invasion for two thousand years. Another argument was that by building the line in the south, that freed additional manpower resources for the north. Again a strange argument since the stated policy of building the line was to provide for defensive warfare.

When the crisis finally exploded in 1939 and France and Britain declared war on Germany, due to the invasion of Poland, this folly was played out. Belgium mobilized as well, then solemnly declared its intention to remain neutral by strictly forbidding *the French and the English* from setting foot on their soil. Any action by the Allies would be construed by the Belgians as an invasion, the armies would be turned around and Belgium would throw in with the Germans. The French couldn't even go to a forward defense on the border with Belguim and Germany.

Several staff members suggested cutting the Belgians off and starting a crash program of digging in, a poor man's Maginot Line program. No, that would upset the Belgians came the reply, and for the next nine months French and British soldiers marshaled by the millions along the Belgian border and waited for the Germans to attack first so they could rush in. As for the Maginot Line, it was properly manned but even the French assumed that the Germans would not attack along this front, and in some sectors supplies and equipment were stripped out to feed the buildup to the north.

The debacle was swift and certain when it hit. On May 10, 1940 the Germans struck along the Belgian border and later that day the Belgians finally gave permission for the Allies to come to their rescue. (Leave it to the French to have such neighbors. Perhaps they should have told the Belgians where to go and what to do while going there.) As it was, the German plan was brilliantly de-

signed around the assumption that the allies would attempt a "Belgian rescue."

The Allies rushed in, the Germans waited several days
for them to get their heads firmly in the noose, then
launched an attack through the Ardennes, north of the
Maginot Line, sliced behind the Allied armies, and raced
to the sea. The entire northern sector in Belgium was cut
off and the Allies lost hundreds of thousands of men,
while several hundred thousand more were evacuated out
of Dunkirk.

Reorganizing after this stunning victory the Germans
raced southward, taking Paris on June 10. A week later
the French signed an armistice and bailed out of the war.

The Maginot Line? Well it did live up to its reputation
as a position that no one would want to storm frontally.
It had an almost fantastic quality to it in that the position
was so well built in places that no one would dream to
attack it, but since it was so well built the French kept
hoping and praying the stupid Germans would attack in
order to justify all the money spent.

The Germans were only too happy to oblige. After
swinging all the way through France, some German units
did finally approach it—from the wrong direction. Of
course, most of the heavy weapons were pointing in the
wrong direction as well!

Rather humanely the Germans tried to coax the defenders out without a fight and in most cases the French
were more than glad to give up. In a few cases, though,
suicidal honor prevailed and the defenders challenged the
Germans to come in and get them. The German response
was tragic and efficient. They brought up some heavy
construction equipment and simply bulldozed shut all the
entrances, ventilation shafts, view ports, and firing slits.

And thus the Maginot Line became a vast tomb. A remarkable story did surface afterwards. Several years after the war a French construction crew was cutting through part of the old line in order to build a highway. They uncovered a shaft and out staggered half a dozen men who had survived underground for seven years! Most of their company had succumbed to madness and suicide. The survivors had sustained themselves on a diet of canned food, stockpiles of cheese and a vast underground wine cellar. They had been declared legally dead and their return from the grave was a cause celebre, as the unsuspecting wife of one of the men had already remarried.

As for the multibillion dollar investment today, one of the original intents of the Line is still functioning: it makes a great wine cellar. Local farmers, as well, have come up with an excellent idea which seems appropriate . . . they've packed sections of the Line with manure and now grow mushrooms.

BUSHIDO POLITICS

Starting a War They Knew
They Could Not Win
1941 Japan

by William R. Forstchen

Sometimes propaganda is so good, it even deludes the propagandists. The Japanese decision to go to war with America in 1941 is a classic example of such delusion.

The history of Japanese military prowess is well known, hearkening back to the legendary age of the samurai warriors. However, forced to confront the growing technological might of the West, Japan embarked on an aggressive program of modernization in order to stay competitive and then stunned the entire world by soundly defeating a Western power, Russia, in the 1904–05 Russo-Japanese War. Several years later Japan struck an alliance with England regarding naval forces in the Pacific, allowing the Royal Navy to concentrate in home waters in preparation for the conflict with Germany, and throughout World War I remained a loyal ally of the West. When it came to dividing up the postwar pie the Allies made a big mistake when they forgot about Japan's assistance. The Japanese ambassadors sent to Versailles presented, to Western eyes, a bizarre and amusing sight; diminutive Orientals wearing diplomats' morning coats and top hats. Dismissed as being an amusing but third-rate ally they were tossed a couple of tidbits as a reward, former German colonies such as Truk and the Gilbert Islands, and unceremoniously sent away from the negotiations being carried on by the real men.

The navy build-down treaties of the 20s were a further insult, with Japan forced into an agreement that limited the size of their ships and insisted that their numbers be significantly less than the American and British navies, the Western argument being that Japan should only be concerned with the Pacific. Further insult was added when Japanese diplomatic overtures regarding an occupation of Manchuria were greeted with a sharp and rapid condemnation from former allies. America evolved a "protective" stance regarding China, due to its missionary involvement throughout the nineteenth and early twentieth centuries, and argued that everyone should allow the Chinese the right of self-determination, and stay out of Manchuria.

For Japan this seemed to be hypocrisy of the worst kind. Only a generation before, Great Britain, France, Germany, and even minuscule Belgium, had engaged in colonization of the worst kind, arbitrarily running amok throughout the world, surveyors in tow, staking out claims to "protective mandates," and "spheres of influence." As for America, it had not hesitated to provoke a war with Spain, then grab up the last vestiges of Hispanic glory in the Pacific. The initial surprise of the Japanese hardened, into a cold and lasting resentment.

In 1930 Soviet troops occupied Manchuria briefly over

a dispute about railroad rights of way, but had then with-drawn. In 1931, regardless of condemnation or approval, Japan staged a coup in Manchuria and, within several months, occupied the iron- and coal-rich province, placing a puppet government in control. Japan would argue that this move was to forestall Soviet expansionism but the argument was not accepted in the West.

China's turn came several years later. Japan used the old technique of declaring that troops were moving in as a protective measure against anarchy to invade China. A three-way war exploded between Nationalist Chinese, Communist Chinese, and Japanese forces. When it came to outside public opinion, especially in America, however, Japan proved to be its own worst enemy.

Japan badly violated the protectiveness America felt for China when it attacked the city of Nanking in 1937. The Japanese general in charge granted to his troops the medieval right of a three-day pillage and rape of the city. More than a quarter of a million civilians died in the anar-chy that followed. American missionaries and their charges witnessed the brutal assault and some of them, armed with cameras, photographed the carnage. In what became a classic example of the power of modern media, American public opinion, though still hobbled by isola-tionism, hardened against Japan when church groups cir-culated the photographs, the new *Life* magazine ran extensive coverage, and newsreel footage was shown in theaters.

Under pressure from America, Japan backed off from a full conquest of China, assuming a less aggressive stance, and there the matter rested for several years. But even as the U.S. began to dislike Japan, something happened to play a major part in forming the Japanese stand on the U.S.—the *Panay* Incident.

On December 12, 1937 Japanese planes attacked an American gunboat, the *Panay*, anchored in the river near Nanking. A number of American sailors died. (The father of the first man to walk on the moon, Neil Armstrong, was one of the survivors.) Japan later apologized and paid an indemnity, but both sides knew the attack was deliberate. It had been a test of nerves and to Japanese thinking it was obvious that America lacked the stomach for a fight.

Opinion now hardened in Japan that it was time for "its place in the sun," and thus they made what seemed to be a series of intelligent and timely moves. The other great powers had seized colonies and it now had the right to do so as well, as any great power had such a right throughout history. Two schools of thought now evolved in the Japanese military, the "Northern School," and the "Southern School."

The Northern School, dominated by the army, argued for renewed pushes in China, and an aggressive war against Russia. The vast resources of Siberia awaited and there were even lofty dreams of one day reaching into the oil fields of Central Asia. This school's arguments were blunted, however, by the stiff Russian response to two border incidents with Soviet forces on the Manchurian border in 1938 and 1939. The pitifully inadequate Japanese armor was trashed by heavier Russian equipment, and the Japanese forces were driven back with heavy casualties. In addition some unexpected fallout from the German-Soviet nonaggression pact of 1939 meant that the Japanese backed away from a confrontation with the Soviet Union, for fear of German reprisal.

The Southern School now gained dominance; its main

goal was colonization. Oil and rubber were waiting to be taken in the Dutch East Indies and French Indochina. As war exploded in Europe, the prizes became even more tempting as the French and Dutch stripped their military forces for defense of the homelands. If the oil fields of the Dutch East Indies could be taken, unlimited fuel would be available for the fleet, and perhaps even the crown jewel of England, India itself, might fall under Japanese control.

And here was the moment of decision, the moment their sensible concept faltered. There was but one force to block them . . . America. It is made even more ironic in light of the fact that thousands of young Japanese men had been coming to America since the start of the century for university training. Even the grand architect of Japanese naval strategy, the legendary Yamamoto, had traveled extensively in the States.

Hitler had declared that America was weak since it was a mongrel amalgamation of races, driven mad by sensationalism, Hollywood, and jazz and jitterbug music. The Japanese, captivated by their own racial theories and tradition of warrior superiority, convinced themselves that Americans would shy away from a fight to the death. Corrupted by their own wealth they would, at best, make a token fight, then quickly concede the western Pacific to whomever wanted to take it. Bushido, the way of the sword, was unknown to Americans. The training, the discipline of Bushido, the willingness to face an opponent blade to blade was part of the warrior mentality of Japan, while the Americans would flee when confronted with such a challenger.

The Southern School won out and plans were developed for a push for colonies in the southern Pacific region.

Within days after the collapse of the French government in 1940, the Japanese navy had made a show of force along the coast of French Indochina. By September 1940 Japan had established airfields on French Vichy territory and America imposed a steel embargo. The American government declared that if the Japanese tried for a full occupation of Indochina, with its vast supply of rubber, America, acting as the OPEC of 1940, would turn off the oil supply.

Late in the spring of 1941 Japan made its move, occupying the rest of Indochina, and America responded as they had stated by turning off the oil. The line had been crossed and both sides knew it.

Japan had amassed an oil reserve stockpile, but in less than a year its military machine would grind to a halt unless the oil fields of the East Indies were secured. The Southern School had forced the government into a head-on collision with America.

And it seemed like the right thing to do. Nearly all the men who planned this strategy had come of age in the glorious war against Russia in 1904–05. That war had opened with a surprise assault on Russian ground and naval forces in the Port Arthur region. Seizing crucial ground and bases, and destroying the Russian Pacific fleet in the opening blow, the Japanese had then waited for the second strike, the arrival of the Russian Baltic fleet. This fleet was annihilated at the Battle of Tsushima, and the Russians sued for peace, conceding that the fight was no longer worth it.

This model was now applied to the war plans against America. In the opening surprise move, the American Pacific fleet would be destroyed at Pearl Harbor. While offensive strikes took over the Dutch East Indies, other forces would seize the remaining American bases in the Pacific and pin American forces in the Philippines. The remains of the American fleet, including its Atlantic units would be forced to come to the aid of its beleaguered forces near Manila, and in a final climactic battle would be destroyed. Faced now with a foe holding fortified bases ringing the western Pacific, its entire fleet decimated, America would lose the will and the interest in fighting, and retreat back to its decadent isolationism.

It seemed like a good idea, on paper at least, and it is stunning that they actually believed in it. Even Yamamoto had his doubts, since he personally knew many of his counterparts in the American navy. With at least this partial knowledge of American character he did insist on one key proviso to the plan. It could be a surprise attack, but several hours before the attack was launched, a formal declaration had to be presented to the American government. He knew enough about us to realize that Americans didn't quite play by the same rules, and had a strange sense of ethics and honor when it came to giving a foe a "sucker punch." If war was first declared, even if only a couple of hours before the attack so that strategic surprise was not lost, then later American public opinion would not be as enraged, and in turn they would be more willing to agree to peace.

There was intense debate about this. War, after all, was war and in the Eastern school of thought the surprise attack was a time-honored tradition, in fact it was expected as a norm. Here the inability of Eastern thinking to penetrate Western logic was clearly evident, the irony being that there were enough Western-educated men in the government and military to issue a warning.

Propaganda had honestly convinced them that Americans were too decadent to respond effectively. Most of all they lacked Bushido, the warrior code of honor, discipline, and, above all else, self-sacrifice.

And so the attack was launched, one of the most brilliant assaults in history. Coordinated across an area encompassing nearly one-sixth of the Earth's surface, Japanese land, air and naval forces struck simultaneously at dozens of targets, gaining nearly complete surprise on all fronts. The momentum thus gained triggered a rout of all who opposed them.

It also cost them the war. The military plan was flawless. The one department that failed completely, however, was the diplomatic one. The declaration breaking diplomatic relations and announcing hostilities was tied up due to a third-rate coding system. Rather than being delivered prior to the assault, it arrived hours after the attacks had already begun and the response is now legendary. Upon hearing of this gaff Yamamoto supposedly declared, "I fear that all we have done is to awaken the sleeping giant."

Yet even if the declaration had arrived prior to the attack, never in the history of modern diplomacy and warfare has there been so profound a misreading of national wills. America did not throw its forces into a desperate relief of the Philippines as the Japanese assumed they would. Rather than risk what was left of the fleet, as the Russians did at Tsushima, the American navy had already decided, if need be, to let the Philippines fall; to then build up an irresistible force and come in strong.

Thus the Japanese were forced to launch an offensive outside the protective cover of ground-based aircraft, venturing into the waters around Midway with the intent of drawing out the American fleet for a final confrontation.

The confrontation was indeed joined. According to reports, the Japanese carrier commander, Nagumo, was stunned by the ferocity of the American attack and stood awestruck as he witnessed the suicidal courage of American pilots pressing the attack regardless of loss. Turning to an aide he supposedly gasped, "My God, these Americans *do* have Bushido."

Most certainly. At the end of the day four Japanese carriers, the backbone of their fleet, were at the bottom of the Pacific. Everything that came afterwards was anticlimactic. The weak Americans, who were supposed to throw in the towel after the second and final defeat, went on to level the cities of Japan as payback for the folly of their believing their enemy would fold. America had no real concept of fighting a limited war and conceding with anything less than total victory. Beyond that, many historians effectively argue that, if anything, the Roosevelt administration was actually baiting the Japanese into a fight as a means of bringing about our involvement in the European war. In some ways the Japanese actually did exactly what the American administration wanted them to do. And the final irony: if the Northern School had prevailed, America might never have entered the war, Stalin never would have been able to transfer his Siberian divisions to Moscow, and today an Axis power could have ruled the Eurasian land mass.

"WE THOUGHT IT WOULD BE SINGAPORE"

U.S. Military High Command Underestimates Japanese Plans 1941 Pearl Harbor

By Brian M. Thomsen

By December of 1941, tensions had been rising between Japan and the United States for over a decade. President Franklin Delano Roosevelt had always been wary of Japanese expansionism, and its steady encroachment on Chinese territories only exacerbated the situation. At the time America was its main supplier of iron, steel, and oil, and Japan was therefore reluctant to completely alienate them until they had secured new sources for these raw materials.

Tensions had been escalating since September 1940, when Japan had entered into the Triple Alliance with Italy and Germany, and had begun to expand its forces into northern Indochina. A U.S. embargo on aviation oil, scrap metal, steel, and iron, was met with Japan's further seizure of the rest of Indochina, to which the United States countered by closing the Panama Canal to all Japanese shipping.

In October of 1941, General Hideki Tojo, leader of the Japanese pro-war party, became premier. Both sides knew that war was inevitable, but nonetheless negotiations toward a peaceful resolution of their problems went on in Washington.

On November 25, 1941, though continuing to negotiate with the U.S., the Japanese premier dispatched aircraft carriers eastward toward Hawaii while also ordering troops to mass along the Malayan border. On December 6, Roosevelt made a final appeal to the Japanese emperor to maintain peace, but his plea fell on deaf ears. However, Roosevelt had been advised on all levels of the U.S. military command that *obviously* Japan would attack Singapore first since this would leave the U.S. with the politically unpopular choice of whether to declare war in order to aid Britain in the defense of her Asian colonies, despite not having been directly attacked. This would undoubtedly be their course of action, and all of the advisors awaited it patiently.

When two Oahu-based U.S. radar operators, who had decided to put in some overtime, reported on December 7 at roughly 0700 that a Japanese strike force was approaching, their observations were disregarded by a junior officer who was sure that there must have been some sort of mistake. Likewise the high command at Pearl Harbor base thought it was totally unnecessary to order a "high state of readiness," or an "alert" status, because they mistakenly believed that they have been kept fully informed by intelligence. No evidence had pointed toward Pearl Harbor as a specific and imminent target. Even though it was known in the U.S. that a Japanese agent in Honolulu had been asked for a report on the Pacific fleet that was stationed there, no significance was attached to this request as similar requests for similar information were intercepted at other locations.

After all, everyone in Washington was sure that Japan would make its point to the United States by attacking Singapore.

As a result, the dawn of December 7, 1941, found Pearl Harbor base the same as any previous day. It was Sunday. Officers and crew from the ships in port were ashore. Aircraft were parked on the airfield wingtip to wingtip, and few antiaircraft guns were manned since most of their ammunition was kept elsewhere under lock and key in accordance with usual peacetime practices. There weren't even any torpedo nets in place to protect the fleet anchorage. Because Pearl Harbor was safe.

The unthinkable and wholly unexpected attack was staged in two waves.

The first wave hit Pearl Harbor at 7:55 A.M. on December 7, 1941; the second wave hit an hour later. The Japanese had sent in six carriers, *Akagi, Kaga, Hiryu, Soryu, Zuikaku,* and *Shokaku,* with a total of 423 planes, each piloted by a flier with weeks of brilliant training. By 9:45 the mission was over, and the planes were returning to the carriers. Most of the American planes on Oahu were decimated; eight battleships, three destroyers, and three cruisers were put out of action; and two battleships, *Oklahoma* and *Arizona* were utterly destroyed. Over two thousand American servicemen were killed.

The Japanese lost a total of 29 aircraft.

Admiral Kimmel, Commander in Chief U.S. Pacific fleet, and General Short, commander of U.S. Army forces in Hawaii, were quickly dismissed from their duties for providing the Japanese strike force with such an easy and defenseless target at Pearl Harbor.

The Americans were saved only by dumb luck: the three carriers serving with the Pacific fleet were all absent at the time of the attack, and likewise the base installations at Pearl Harbor, including massive oil-storage tanks, escaped unscathed.

Thus, though the American fleet was crippled, it was nonetheless left with a base from which it could rebuild, a process that was begun immediately after the day that President Roosevelt referred to as "a day that will live in infamy."

One final note—Singapore fell to the Japanese on February 15, 1942, the attack by Japan having commenced on the day after the attack on Pearl Harbor.

LOYAL TO A FAULT

Declare War on Who, Mein Führer?
1941 Germany

by William R. Forstchen

It was the first week of December 1941, the most fateful week of the Second World War. Most Americans, when reading about Pearl Harbor's "day of infamy" responded to it by running to enlist. President Roosevelt declared that December 7 was a "date which will live in infamy," and congress voted to declare war on Japan. But only Japan, no mention of a war against Germany was ever made. This is why the later decisions made by the Führer of the German Reich, Adolf Hitler, were so clearly wrong.

How did Germany end up facing the Americans? They had enjoyed a nearly unbroken string of successes. First Poland, then Norway, Denmark, the Low Countries, France, Greece, the Balkan states, and most of western Russia had fallen to the unrelenting power of the German blitzkrieg. There had been but two reversals up till this point—the air assault on England, which had failed to pave the way for a seaborne attack, and a minor reversal in the sideshow of North Africa, forcing Rommel's small force back from its drive on Alexandria.

In Russia the campaign had been unstoppable. Most of the Ukraine, that all-important breadbasket and industrial heart of the Soviet empire, had fallen. Leningrad was all but surrounded and starving, and advanced elements of German armor were within sight of the Kremlin. The killing blow against Moscow could have been delivered in September, but the forces originally committed to Moscow were diverted by order of Hitler to storm into the flank of the Russian army in the northern Ukraine and encircle it. The greatest mass capitulation in the history of warfare resulted in nearly 700,000 Soviet troops going into captivity. Needless to say, such a victory was a clear signal that the lightning strike into the heart of Russia was all but completed. With the fall of Moscow, the political and societal desire to continue the futile resistance would surely collapse in a coup against Stalin.

This encircling drive delayed that final offensive. By the time the triumphant German armies had repositioned themselves, the coldest winter in over fifty years was settling over Russia, with temperatures plummeting to more than forty below zero. The German army was ill-equipped for such conditions, having anticipated that the campaign would be over before the hard freeze of winter set in, and now struggled to survive as it advanced. And then, starting on December 5, in the suburbs of Moscow, the Wehrmacht ran into elements of dozens of divisions which German intelligence believed were still six thousand miles away, guarding the uneasy border between Japanese-occupied Manchuria and Soviet Siberia. But they were wrong. The powerful and highly trained Siberian army had arrived to save Moscow.

On the same day that the planes of the Japanese navy struck Pearl Harbor another attack was sprung half a world away as the full fury of the Siberian divisions was unleashed. The German offensive on Moscow was stopped in its tracks.

Now unfold the misguided plans that culminated in the turning of the tide of World War II. Early in the war a series of meetings had been held between Germany and Japan, with Germany aggressively seeking an alliance that could tie down British and French assets in the Pacific. Hitler, as well, attempted to maneuver the Japanese into striking at Russia through Siberia. In Japan there was some sentiment, particularly from the army, for this idea. But in the end, the navy won the argument for offensive action against America. It was a decision they never bothered to convey to their German allies, though Stalin did learn about Japanese intentions through a well-placed spy in Tokyo, thus allowing him to start an immediate withdrawal of Siberian troops toward Moscow once the Germans attacked.

Once the offensive against Russia had started the German Foreign Minister, von Ribbentrop, repeatedly conveyed to the Japanese that Siberia was theirs for the taking, but the requests for their involvement were met with silence, and the plans for the strike on Pearl Harbor moved forward. Nearly all the German high command were caught completely by surprise with the news that the Japanese had attacked America and Britain. At least regarding Great Britain, it was welcome news; it ensured that significant resources of the Commonwealth would now be committed to yet another theater of operations. But when it came to America, the top German planners held their breaths.

America, still dominated by isolationist sentiment, had stayed out of direct involvement in the conflict. American supplies, under the lend-lease program, were flooding into Britain and the Soviet Union. Only the month before, American troops had even been dispatched to Iceland, and there had been several encounters between U-boats and American destroyers, but the potential might of an aroused United States had not been thrown into the European conflict.

The reaction of most of Hitler's advisors to the Japanese attack was mixed. There was nearly universal frustration with the Japanese failure to go along with an attack on Russia. (In fact, for the next four years Japan and Russia maintained diplomatic contact and, though a neutral power in that conflict, Russia actually interned any American flyers who touched down in their territory after strikes against Japanese targets.) Until Roosevelt's speech the day after the attack most Germans were fearful that the president would find the Japanese attack to be an excuse to declare war on Germany as well. After Roosevelt's speech, the feeling was that at least indirectly the Japanese attack might prove to be a blessing, fixating American attention on the Pacific.

And then, on December 11, Hitler declared war on America.

Von Ribbentrop and nearly all of Hitler's advisors were thunderstruck. Why declare war on America? The Russians had suddenly proven to have a second wind, Britain had yet to be cowed, and as for the Japanese, they had proven to be a faithless and self-serving ally. They refused to strike Russia in a coordinated attack, which freed the Siberian divisions to wreak havoc upon the icebound divisions now stuck in front of Moscow.

The man who had once dismissed treaties as "mere scraps of paper," now suddenly proved to have scruples. Hitler declared that there was indeed an "understanding" between Japan and Germany. Since Japan, a good friend whom he once described as the Aryan race of the Pacific, had embarked on a war with America, Germany was honor bound to follow. As reports of the damage to Pearl Harbor, and the vast, sweeping scope of the Japanese offensive, which stretched from Indonesia to the Central Pacific, filtered in, Hitler expressed unstinting admiration for the skill and cunning of the Japanese and prophesied that Japan would dictate peace terms in San Francisco.

He was reminded of how crucial the American intervention had been in World War I, especially the flood of American supplies to the French and British armies. It was also pointed out that, except for a few dozen U-boats, Germany had absolutely no means of striking in any way whatsoever at the United States. If need be America could sit back for years and build up a massive force which, once unleashed, would be unstoppable.

His advisors had fallen victim to American propaganda, Hitler raged in reply. The Japanese understood that weakness and were now exploiting it. America was a nation corrupted by money and "Jewish influences." Its youth were soft weaklings and would never fight, being addicted to jitterbug dancing. Now, he declared, was the time to eliminate America as well.

In desperation it was pointed out that the situation on the Moscow front was rapidly deteriorating. But Hitler considered that was only a temporary reversal, he scorned the idea of getting the troops out to rebuild for a renewed spring offensive.

His ensuing "stand fast" orders commanded that all

250 IT SEEMED LIKE A GOOD IDEA

German units were to stay in place against the onslaught of the Siberian troops.

The following spring Germany did renew its offensive on Russia but the striking power of 1941 was gone forever. During the winter the Wehrmacht had sustained over a million casualties, a fair percentage of them due to frostbite, in order to hold the frozen ground west of Moscow. The ability to strike toward Leningrad, Moscow, and the eastern Ukraine could not be sustained so Hitler decided on a drive to the oil fields beyond the Ukraine. It reached only as far as Stalingrad. And while this renewed German offensive was mired on the banks of the Volga, troops waded ashore in North Africa, the vanguard of an army, eight million strong, that had abandoned its "addiction" to jitterbugging in order to carve the heart out of fascism.

The twin decisions to stand fast in Russia and declare war on America might have sounded good at the time, and in fact they were . . . for they turned the tide of the war.

THE OTHER MAGINOT LINE

Germany and the West Wall
1944 Germany

by William R. Forstchen

A week after breaking out of the Ardennes north of the French Maginot Line, German armor columns came to a halt on the bluffs looking out over the English Channel. They had accomplished one of the greatest feats of arms in the history of modern warfare. Less than three weeks later France capitulated. England stood alone, and throughout that fateful summer and fall of 1940 braced for an invasion that never came.

Two years later the situation had changed drastically. Having considered England to be a minor annoyance, who would soon collapse, Hitler turned east to destroy the Soviet Union. It was now late 1942, a German army was dying in Stalingrad, another was reeling back from the British onslaught at El Alamein, and American troops were sweeping up the coast of western North Africa. It was evident that sooner or later, perhaps in less than a year, the Allies would attempt to force the English Channel and retake France by storm.

The Maginot Line stands as a classic example of misguided defense and is an easy target for teasing the French. The Germans, however, built their own Maginot Line which was, in terms of total industrial output, even more extensive and expensive than the French effort, and chose a strategic path that was a disaster. Yet few historians (Stephen Ambrose being one of the few exceptions) have ever called them to task for what seemed quite clever at the time. Perhaps this is a result of the fact that the chief architect of this supreme folly was Erwin Rommel.

Rommel is a name that is still associated with the most brilliant tactical and operational victories in the history of the Nazi war effort. He is accepted as well as being somewhat of a palatable enemy, a gallant knight of the old school trapped alongside a gallery of rogues. Politically he is safe to praise as well since he did work to overthrow Hitler in 1944, and might very well have been appointed military dictator if the plot had succeeded, but was forced to commit suicide when caught by the Gestapo.

The mere fact that he endorsed a plan and aggressively pushed it, tends to create the impression that it must have been one hell of a good idea but just not applied forcefully enough. Of course, Hitler probably screwed it up as well. That wasn't necessarily the case.

After the collapse of the German war effort in North Africa in the winter of 1942–43, Rommel was recalled to Germany, supposedly for treatment of a sinus infection, but actually to spare Germany the humiliation of losing their most famous field marshal in a lost cause. After recovering from his illness he was finally summoned to a meeting with his Führer, and was there given the task of preparing defenses in France and the Low Countries for an Allied invasion that might come as early as 1943.

This West Wall, as it was dubbed, was being touted by Goebbels and the Nazi propaganda machine as an already impregnable line of fortifications. Rommel accepted the position, but the byzantine system of command gave him little direct operational control in a situation that would require a single unified command if and when the invasion finally came.

And now we see why this plan, which was actually pretty stupid, was allowed to continue. Rommel actually embraced the concept of the West Wall, and publicly declared that the battle of the invasion would be decided "at the water's edge."

He threw himself wholeheartedly into the effort and working in tandem with Albert Speer, director of armaments, managed to gain a high priority level for important strategic materials, especially concrete. The conditions that Rommel discovered on his first inspection tour of the West Wall left him appalled. Except for some showcase fortresses around the Pas de Calais area, the section of the French coast at the narrowest point of the Channel, little if any work had been done.

During the next year Rommel mobilized hundreds of thousands of troops, most of them third-rate units made up of overage and underage men and boys, disabled veterans from Russia, and recruits from Poland and Russia. He placed all his resources into the creation of beachfront fortifications. Hundreds of thousands of steel obstacles designed to rip up landing craft were strewn like jacks along more than two thousand miles of oceanfront. His demand for land mines was insatiable. He asked for a million, then two million, and strove for a goal of twelve million. Elaborate fortresses, more heavily reinforced than anything on the Maginot Line, were built, designed to withstand a direct hit from a sixteen-inch artillery shell fired from a battleship. Behind the lines hundreds of thousands of telephone poles, known as "Rommel's asparagus," were planted in fields that might be potential landing sites for gliders. The equivalent of billions of dollars of resources were poured into the project . . . and the entire thing was a vast mistake, made historically acceptable to some because it was the great Rommel who ordered it so.

One should consider the actual results achieved. Most of the effort went into the Pas de Calais region, and it can be argued that so effective were the fortifications that it deterred the Allies from landing there. If this is true the Germans should have realized it as well and cast a more careful eye as to what would be the next most likely site—Normandy.

Rommel had declared that the Allies would attempt to land at high tide, thus the liberal strewing of obstacles and traps between the high- and low-tide marks. Never was it seriously considered that the Allies might be willing to risk a low-tide landing and attempt to storm the couple of hundred meters of open beach, which is exactly what they did. Thus tens of thousands of tons of precious steel were wasted.

As for the fortifications, the problem with defensive works is that one must fortify all points, but the enemy can then pick and choose the best striking point. Like an earthen dam in a flood, all that is needed is for a tiny hole, no more than the width of a finger, to be carved

through and all the remaining millions of tons of earth
are quickly swept away.

The only place along the entire sixty miles of beaches
where the Allies encountered truly serious resistance was
at Omaha, where several thousand casualties were taken
before the beach and the bluffs beyond were finally
cleared. Once the holes were punched at Omaha and the
other four landing sites, there was essentially a defensive
vacuum except for the natural advantages offered by the
hedgerow country.

The German West Wall probably ranks in the top ten
all-time colossal failures. The French have taken a lot of
heat through the years for the folly of the Maginot Line,
but in defense of the French it could at least be said that
the Line was indeed so impressive that the Germans bypassed it. Nowhere was it directly assaulted and seriously
breached in battle. The much-vaunted German army held
for less than a half day. And even if they had indeed
thrown back the assault at Omaha, an impossible consideration not just due to the firepower from offshore but
also due to the sheer guts of the GIs assaulting the position, the lodgments gained on the other four beaches
would have won through in the end anyhow. Once those
lodgments were made, all the millions of tons of concrete
and steel deployed elsewhere became nothing but scrap
and junk.

It's almost as if Rommel had set out on a deliberate
policy to divert essential resources. Many historians argue
that if only Rommel had been given clear command, if
only he had been at the front that morning and been able
to launch a true counteroffensive, he might very well have
driven the invasion back into the sea. Others argue that

Rommel was right and, as usual, it was Hitler who screwed it all up. Rubbish.

The most remarkable point of this entire good idea is that it was Rommel, the master of maneuver, the point man for the German offensive of 1940, the one who had scoffed at the misguidedness of the Maginot Line, who in the end built the biggest defensive white elephant of all.

The one German armor unit that did counterattack late on D-Day was torn to shreds by allied naval gunfire and air attack. This lends strength to the argument of those few who dared to challenge Rommel, to concede the beaches to an Allied force that had overwhelming power at the water's edge. All of the concrete should have been used, instead, to build defensive works further back, at key positions the Allies would have to attack no matter where they landed, and far out of range of naval gunfire support. It was even argued that the concrete should have been used for the making of more strategic highways to free movement up from the far more vulnerable rail lines. The hundreds of thousands of static troops manning the coastal defenses should have been positioned inland instead. Heavy barriers of fortifications around the Ruhr, and along the Oder on the Russian front, might very well have delayed, perhaps even stopped the Allied offensives.

The entire point is moot, though, for if Germany had managed to drag the war out another half a year, it would have been Berlin rather than Hiroshima that received the first atomic bomb. So perhaps, for the sake of the Germans, Rommel's decision was a good idea after all.

IN EXCHANGE FOR NOTHING

Roosevelt Gives Away the Store
1945 Yalta

By Bill Fawcett

When Winston Churchill, Joseph Stalin, and Franklin Roosevelt met in Yalta, a small city located in the newly liberated Crimea, they never expected that World War II would end within a matter of months. Germany was still fighting and the Battle of the Bulge had occurred less than two months earlier. Each man had his own concerns. Stalin was watching the desperate defense of the Reich further cripple his already depleted manpower. Russia had lost over twenty million people to the war and had suffered proportionally far more than even France. Churchill was concerned with Europe, Communism, and the Near East. And Roosevelt, well, he had the most pressing problems.

While Japan was being forced back to their main islands, there was no sign at all of a lessening in the fanatic resistance shown by Japanese forces. The Kamikaze had sent naval casualties soaring, and the bloody defense of

Okinawa boded very badly for projected casualties in future battles. The next step in the war against Japan, featur-
ing almost entirely American forces, was the actual
invasion of the Japanese islands themselves. Based on earlier battles against Japanese-held islands, American casualties were projected to be as many as half a million. This
estimate took into account the hundreds of Kamikaze aircraft known to be waiting and the general population,
trained with spears for human-wave attacks against the
invaders.

The atomic bomb, known as the Manhattan Project,
gave some hope, but at this time no one was even sure
the bomb would work. It would be several months and a
new president later before that was a viable alternative to
a grinding invasion. So while Stalin looked to Europe, and
particularly eastern Europe, and Churchill worried about
Stalin and how to end the European War as decisively
and quickly as possible, Franklin Roosevelt had to put
gaining Russian assistance in the war against Japan as a
top priority.

The apparent need for Russian assistance, meaning
Russian bodies to absorb some of the horrendous casualties expected in the invasion of the home islands, was a
constant and compelling factor in the Yalta Declaration
that resulted from the weeklong meeting. This agreement
recognized the three occupation zones for Germany (the
French were included later, at Potsdam), and set the terms
for Germany's surrender, including massive reparations
for the Russians. But Roosevelt's desire to sway the Russians is seen in the concessions granted: the Declaration
virtually legalized the Russian control of the nations they
occupied in the interest of the "establishment of order in
Europe," and specifically granted Russia direct adminis-

tration of Poland until a "democratic government" could
be put in place. There had to be little question in Churchill
or Roosevelt's mind as to what type of government would
be elected in the Russian-occupied territories. In exchange
for legitimizing Stalin's payload of all of eastern Europe,
with a few islands north of Japan thrown in for good
measure, Stalin agreed that within "ninety days of the
end of the War in Europe" Russia would declare war on
Japan (it never had, even after Pearl Harbor) and presum-
ably join in the invasion of the Japanese home islands.
Roosevelt got his promise of an allied invasion army and
Stalin in exchange got de facto domination of half of
Europe.

The invasion of Japan was never to occur. The two
atomic bombs dropped at Hiroshima and Nagasaki
brought the Pacific War to an abrupt end on the battleship
Missouri. It turned out that Russia never had to move even
a single soldier to the east, toward Japan. Yet as per the
agreement the dictatorial and eventually bankrupt Communist Party was to control over 100 million residents of
eastern Europe in what will probably stand as the last,
great nationalistic empire. The Yalta Declaration was most
certainly the best deal Stalin ever made. And as for the
100 million people who suffered almost fifty years under
repressive Communist puppet states, all we can say was
that at the time, to President Franklin D. Roosevelt, it
seemed like the way to go.

DOCUMENTED FOR POSTERITY

Nazi Documentary Evidence Presented
at the Nuremberg Trials
1945–46 Germany

By Brian M. Thomsen

Blinded by gas in 1918, Adolf Hitler swore that if he recovered his sight he would abandon his plans to become an architect and enter politics. When his sight returned he vowed that he would bring Germany from the depths of despair to the greatness she deserved. But Hitler's plan contained an unusual twist.

More than any previous madman, Hitler was a demagogue of the twentieth century and, as a result, was committed to capturing for posterity all of the brilliance of his work in progress, ordering his high command to keep meticulous records so that later generations would be able to not just bask in his glory, but appreciate the work of those under him as well. Needless to say, men with names like Goering, Himmler, and Speer were more than agreeable to share in this glory.

Hitler and his propaganda minister, Joseph Goebbels, were, however, interested in more than just print records.

Germany was an international center for cutting-edge filmmaking, and its studios in Babelsburg (outside of Potsdam) were the breeding ground for classic films from Fritz Lang (*Metropolis, M,* and *the Mabuse* series, F. W. Murnau (*Nosferatu*), and Robert Wiene (*The Cabinet of Dr. Caligari*). Furthermore, the talented female documentarian, Leni Riefenstahl, had helped to further Nazi propaganda interests with her epics of Aryan mastery *Olympia* and *Triumph of the Will*. Hitler and his ministers were not even content to stop there, but commissioned cameramen to record all aspects of the great Aryan achievements along the way to the "Thousand Year Reich."

Moving film and stills recorded all aspects of the war effort—the factories, the training camps, soldiers being sent out on missions, as well as the rebuilding of Berlin, the arts, and the political rallies. Since racial cleansing and the harvesting of usable detritus from undesirables was also part of the overall plan, cameramen were dispatched to such installations as Dachau, Buchenwald, Treblinka, and Auschwitz, so that an accurate pictorial record could be obtained, preserving the efforts that were expended for the greater glory of Germany.

Once Germany had lost the war and Hitler had committed suicide, an international tribunal was called to try high-ranking Nazi officials for their wartime actions that went beyond accepted laws and practices. These so-called war crimes included, but were not limited to, unrestricted submarine warfare against civilian merchant ships, the use of conscripted slave labor, the looting and decimation of occupied countries, and the abuse and murder of prisoners of war, and civilians, particularly Jews, gypsies, and other non-Aryans.

The tribunal started work on November 20, 1945, in

Nuremberg, Germany, and was administered by a joint Allied task force with representative judges from the U.S., Great Britain, and the Soviet Union, in the true spirit of allied tripartisanship.

While mounting their cases against the Nazi war criminals, eyewitnesses and wronged individuals testified against those on trial. Originally the members of the tribunal were afraid that most of their evidence would exist solely in the form of "he said/she said" testimony. Furthermore, the severity of the inhumanity of the accused actions was constantly being called into question. Death and suffering were considered to be a normal part of war. Was there evidence available that proved that the Nazis had indeed crossed the line?

Thanks to the efforts of Wild Bill Donovan of the OSS, the precursor to the CIA, a steady flow of incriminating documents began to pour in from various archives, including official records from the Nazi high command. Those on trial were destined to be convicted on the basis of the records and documents that they themselves had been so assiduous in compiling.

Thanks to the cinematic interests of Hitler and Goebbels, ample film footage existed of the Reich's efforts and atrocities, much of which was fashioned into documentary evidence in such screened films as *The Nazi Plan* and *Nazi Concentration Camps*, which visually documented to all of the horrified viewers exactly how far the Nazis had gone, leaving none of the atrocities committed to anyone's imagination.

As Hitler well knew, pictures always made more of an impact than words.

By the end of the proceedings, twenty-one Nazi officials were convicted of various war crimes, and of these twelve were sentenced to hang and the remainder were sent to prison. Lesser officials, such as prison guards and civilian collaborators, were then put on trial, resulting in an additional 24 executions and another 128 prison sentences.

Apologists for those on trial argued that it was unlawful to try these individuals for actions that were not considered crimes at the time and in the places that they were committed, but Robert Jackson, Chief Justice of the United States Supreme Court and the chief U.S. prosecutor at the trials, successfully argued that the individuals in question had to be held accountable for their unconscionable actions in order to deter such actions in future aggressions. His argument prevailed and was eventually agreed to and sanctioned by the United Nations.

There were not many disagreements over the actual occurrences of the crimes, and who did what to who— the heinous war crimes had indeed been recorded for posterity, but not in the way that had originally been intended.

KEEP THE COLONY, BUT START A WAR

The Beginnings of Thirty Years of Indochina Warfare 1945 France and America in Indochina

by William R. Forstchen

This collection of "good ideas" would not be complete without a look at the policy-making decisions that dragged two world powers down to humiliating defeat, caused governments to fall, and in the process resulted in well over a million tragic and needless deaths . . . and they are the origins of the Indochina wars.

The political paradigm in the Pacific in 1945 was far more bizarre and complex than most people now realize, and the focal point of that bizarreness was Indochina.

This goes back to France 1940, which, after a disastrous six-week campaign, had gone down to bitter defeat before the German blitzkrieg. Not all of France, however, was occupied, and in actuality France switched sides during the war. Northern France, Paris, and the coastal areas were direct zones of occupation, but the rest of France was now ruled by a collaborative government with its capital in Vichy. From 1940–44 French units around the world would actually fight on the side of the fascist cause. With this ignoble collapse French colonial administrators were forced to make a choice, and in nearly every case they sided with the fascists, at least until an Allied fleet came over the horizon.

Thus, in late 1940, when the Japanese "requested" access to ports and the establishment of airfields in Indochina in order to press its war against China, the Vichy French government was more than happy to comply. In mid-1941 the Japanese invaded Indochina openly and took it all without the slightest resistance. Now comes the truly unusual part of the story . . . for the next four years French administrators, bureaucrats, military personnel, and police forces cooperated fully with the Japanese. They were, in fact, on the side of Japan in the Pacific.

By 1944 the tide had obviously turned in the Pacific. In an interesting and unusual operation, American OSS operatives established contact with Vietnamese nationalists led by Ho Chi Minh and offered logistical support and training. By early 1945 these forces were aggressively operating against Japanese forces in the north of Indochina. At sea British naval forces bombarded Japanese positions and harbor facilities. The French, at this stage, kept a decidedly low profile. Perhaps a key turning point here was the death of Roosevelt who had made a clear statement that, given their record of collaboration, the French had to consider their holdings in Indochina forfeit and that American policy wanted to see a free and independent postwar Indochina. This was similar to the manner in which America had made a commitment to the Philippines for independence within a year after the war ended. This was a crucial commitment to counter Japanese propa-

ganda that they were fighting a war of liberation in the
Orient against Western imperialism.

With the surrender of Japan, significant Japanese
forces were stranded all the way from China, through
Burma, and across Indonesia. This was true in Indochina
as well. Nationalist forces, led by Ho and assisted by
American OSS operatives, swept into Hanoi and with full
approval from their OSS supporters the Nationalists declared a free and independent republic.

This whole period in the history of Vietnam and its
relationship to America is now shrouded in confused in-
terpretations and outright misrepresentations. The question centers on whether Ho was, in fact, already in league
with Stalin and Mao to bring Indochina over to Communism or not. We might never really know the truth of the
matter, but the ensuing weeks certainly stand as a case
study in good plans gone awry.

British troops soon landed in order to provide some
sort of administrative control, to take responsibility for
the tens of thousands of Japanese POWs, and to start the
repatriation process. Ho repeatedly quoted the American
Constitution and the writings of Abraham Lincoln as
models for his country and asked for American assistance
in postwar development of Indochina. His OSS advisors
reported that a socialist Ho could indeed be worked with,
but that the French administration in Indochina was a
corrupt, collaborative government that should be unceremoniously evicted.

And then the French landed.

French troops, including foreign legion units, which
had a heavy sprinkling of new recruits with heavy German accents, landed in Indochina. In this confused period
of transition from American OSS and British control and

assistance over to the French, a truly bizarre and remarkable event occurred. Japanese troops were released from POW holding areas, given back their arms, and sent out into the streets to "maintain control." If ever there was an affront to a nation of people who had allied with the Western cause of freedom, it was here. In order to "police" the very people who had fought for freedom, a brutal former enemy was sent back out to guard them.

The French made some noises about acknowledging the Indochina Republic, but with the proviso that it would be part of a French Commonwealth similar to the British system. Amazingly, and in spite of protests from every top military commander in the field, Truman went along with the French demands for the reoccupation of Indochina until such time as the people were ready for self-determination. Truman stated that DeGaulle had made this a major sticking point in postwar relations with France, and that French national pride demanded that all colonies be returned whether they had collaborated with the enemy or not. It did seem like a sensible way to go, since DeGaulle had pointed out as well that Ho was preparing to throw in with Mao's Communists, who were renewing their efforts for postwar control.

And so the situation stood. American and British support and advisors were pulled out, the French built up their occupation forces (and finally got the Japanese guards out after violent protests from America and Britain), and once they were strong enough the French started to clamp down on Ho and his government. By the end of 1946 Ho abandoned any pretext of working with the French, fled Hanoi, and guerilla warfare resumed.

Since America was now firmly on the side of France, at least publicly buying the French line about Communist

influences, and America was moving toward establishment of the Truman Doctrine, it was inevitable that
America would wind up providing military support to
France's efforts to suppress Ho. Ho, in turn, soon got help
from the only sources possible for weapons and supply,
the Communists in China (who were, in fact, an old traditional enemy of the Vietnamese) and from Stalin. The die
was cast for a thirty-year war, all of it based on the para-
dox of backing a French administration which had fought
against us in World War II, to destroy a nation which
actually had been on our side.

STAND BACK BOYS AND GIVE THE PRESIDENT SOME ROOM

The Secret Service and the Protection of the President
1963 Dallas, Texas

By Brian M. Thomsen

Recent matters in the headlines have highlighted Secret Service agents, the cadre of uniformed and plainclothes guards who make up the Executive Protective Services, and their duty to be at the president's side at all times to assure his protection, which sometimes brings them into direct conflict with the wishes and desires of their charge.

But the Secret Service didn't really start out this way.

Though the Secret Service was signed into being by Abraham Lincoln (ironically, the first American president to be assassinated) in 1865, it was originally charged with investigating counterfeiting, opium smuggling, and extortion and racketeering, as well as other cases that were assigned as needed. Presidents in the late 1800s and early 1900s have also assigned them to espionage investigations during wartime and various cases of land fraud and government corruption in regard to the Homestead Act. Eventually some of these agents were transferred to the

Department of Justice to launch the Federal Bureau of Investigation and assume some of the discretionary investigative duties that had formerly been foisted on the Service.

In 1901 the Secret Service was officially charged with the protection of the president, though Congress did not vote money to pay for this duty until 1906, or make the assignment permanent until 1951, after three U.S. presidents had already been assassinated: Lincoln, Garfield, and McKinley. Prior to this the presidents had been protected by a combination of military guards and private bodyguards. In both cases, these protective units were always deferential to the desires of the chief executive and trained to follow his orders unequivocally.

Presidents, being political animals, usually desired the ability to campaign up close and personal with their constituency, and in the age prior to television and radio this, of course, required face-to-face, large-scale interactions, hand shaking and baby kissing. Likewise, the chief executive usually wanted a certain amount of confidentiality in his dealings with various contacts and advisors. Both of these situations usually resulted in the president ordering his guards to back off so that they would not be perceived as coming between the president and his public, or overhearing conversations that were meant only for certain ears.

Such was the case with William McKinley, who ordered his men to back off one time too many, and was assassinated by anarchist Leon Czolgosz with his guards too far away to intervene.

The charging of the Secret Service with sole responsibility for the protection of the president and his family enabled them to organize a plan of action, and improve it over the years through experience and innovation, in order to assure the safety of the chief executive of the United States of America.

The first change was that the Secret Service was put on duty twenty-four hours a day. When President Wilson was dating Mrs. Edith Bolling Galt, they were there. Likewise when Coolidge was grieving at his dying son's bedside, when Franklin Delano Roosevelt traveled the world during World War II, and when Truman had his late-night poker games. Agents would also be dispatched to go to school with the president's children, accompanying them as they socialized with their friends, even on dates, and even escorted them on their honeymoons, should such closely observed courtships manage to survive the surveillance.

For six decades the service had a perfect record in the execution of its duties. Then came Dallas on November 22, 1963.

John Fitzgerald Kennedy, the thirty-fifth president of the United States, had overcome numerous obstacles on the way to the White House. Both his youth (at the age of forty-three, he was then the youngest man to be elected president via the electoral college) and his religion (Roman Catholic) were thought to be insurmountable factors that would be held against him by the American people. They weren't, leading him to consider himself "the people's choice."

Kennedy's belief in this led to televised tours of the White House, and the development of programs such as the Peace Corps, which were all directed toward the aspirations of the ordinary people, making the masses feel that they were indeed a part of their government.

This way of thinking also led to his decision to break

down some of the traditional barriers between the presidency and the people, and was instrumental in his ordering the removal of Secret Service agents from the corners of his car in the Dallas motorcade on that fateful day in 1963 when he was assassinated. Had agents been present, it is entirely possible that they might have interfered with the sniper's line of sight, or perhaps managed to intervene faster in order to avoid the fatal consequences that followed so quickly.

The president's desire to be more open to the people, to break down the barriers between himself and the masses, and the Secret Service bowing to his wishes, was very likely the cause of his death.

PHILBY—BRITAIN'S BEST AND MOSCOW'S MAN INSIDE

British Spy Defects–Number Two Man
Exposed as Soviet Mole
1963 Moscow

By Brian M. Thomsen

Stewart Menzies seemed an ideal man to run the SIS, the British Secret Intelligence Service. He was well connected in high society, alleged by some to be the illegitimate son of Edward VII, and possessed of great charm, many friends, and a great natural facility for surviving. He also trusted his subordinates to get the job done and so didn't get in their way, letting the department basically run itself. When the time came for him to choose a successor, however, he might have taken a harder look at exactly what his appointee had been doing for too many years.

For Menzies chose an affable fellow by the name of Kim Philby as his heir. Philby, a Cambridge graduate, was considered to be one of the best and the brightest of the professional intelligence men who had served under Menzies during World War II, and was clearly headed for even bigger challenges and responsibilities.

Philby was first sent off to get some field experience in Turkey from 1947 to 1949, and then was posted to the plum position as SIS liaison officer with the CIA and the FBI, and stationed in Washington, D.C.

The Americans welcomed him with open arms, having been wooed by tales of his wartime successes, and were eager to pick his mind for tips he might have picked up during his inaugural tenure at creating SIS's anti-Soviet section. He was given direct access at every level, even to the directors, and all doors were opened to him. His job was to facilitate the exchange of information between the two American intelligence services, the CIA and the FBI, and the two British ones, SIS and MI6, and he threw himself into all of the tasks at hand, immersing himself in the shared intelligence that both sides had gathered.

Menzies only received glowing reports on how his young protégé was doing in the United States, and was personally gratified that he had indeed chosen the right successor.

There was only one problem—Philby was actually working for the other side; not the United States, mind you, but the Soviet Union, the foreign power that he had supposedly become an expert in working against.

While still at University back in 1933, Philby was observed by agents of the OGPU (perhaps by a Cambridge don working in league with them) as being one of a number of young and privileged British intellectuals who were considered to be idealistically sympathetic to the Soviet cause, and approached. When informally pressed to express his views and political theories, he was offered opportunities to assist certain foreign concerns in their philosophical quests. In no time at all, the gloves were taken off and his OGPU recruiters made their intentions more blatant. In Philby's words: "I was recruited in June of 1933, and given the job of penetrating British intelligence and told that it did not matter how long it took to do the job."

In Washington, Philby had quickly established a certain status quo as far as information on British and American intelligence was concerned, providing his controllers with much usable information that would weaken the efforts that he was supposedly supporting, while at the same time never passing on any delicate information that might later be tracked back to him alone, thus avoiding the threat of the exposure of his true allegiances.

Though the actual damage done by Philby through his passing of secrets back to the Soviet Union was quite substantial, the really devastating blow was not so much in regard to operations, but rather in the suspicion that his actions engendered between the American intelligence services and the British. The so-called special relationship of trust that had existed between the two would forever be under a shadow of suspicion, and never again would intelligence agents be able to completely trust even their closest comrades in spying.

Philby never did, however, manage to succeed Menzies as head of SIS. The Foreign Office, whose approval would be necessary should Menzies ever retire and appoint Philby as his successor, had decided to observe him without his knowledge, and discovered him to have acquired a certain shiftiness, and that he seemed to be growing progressively more worried and tense as time went on. Philby had also developed a drinking problem as the pressures of leading a double life seemed to catch up with him. The Foreign Office found him to be unsuitable, but

Menzies insisted that when the time came he would be able to justify Philby's promotion.

Menzies, however, was spared this embarrassment as Philby had to defect before such a promotion could be arranged. While aiding and abetting the defection of Donald MacLean and Guy Burgess, fellow spies within British intelligence who had been exposed as Soviet moles by members of the CIA, Philby wound up putting himself in jeopardy, and barely managed to escape to Moscow himself, years later, after preliminary investigations into his suspicious actions began. Part of the reason for his defection was to protect a fourth spy, Sir Anthony Blunt, who was left in place, and only discovered by British spy catchers years later after he had already been knighted by the queen.

Thus, the best spy SIS had to offer was indeed the best spy that they ever encountered.

THROWING OUT THE BABY AND SAVING THE BATH WATER

The BBC is a Bureaucracy After All
1967 Britain

by Jody Lynn Nye

As a provider of broadcast entertainment, the British Broadcasting Corporation has few peers in terms of quality. For more than seven decades, it has produced and transmitted concerts, documentaries, comedies, children's programming, educational programs, dramatic series, both new and classic plays, and news of a standard admired the world over on radio, television and shortwave.

Licensed by the Post Office as the British Broadcasting Company in 1922, it was intended to provide service "to the reasonable satisfaction of the Postmaster-General," the authority behind the system. Its intentions were excellent. The company endorsed British manufacturers for its radio sets and British labor. The broadcasts were to be commercial free, in order that the content not be tainted by endorsements that would unduly influence the public. Its funding would come directly from its viewers.

In order to receive the BBC services, British listeners,

and later, viewers, had to pay a licensing fee to the Post Office. Initially ten shillings per year, it has grown to over seventy pounds sterling. The BBC's status as a government-supported monopoly kept the playing field of broadcasting to itself for decades. It was many years before independent commercial television companies or radio stations were permitted to occupy airwaves previously ruled by the BBC. Even so, any television sold had to be licensed, whether or not the owner watched the BBC. That fee, plus royalties on sets sold with the BBC seal of approval, and the Grant-in-Aid for the BBC World Service, were the sole sources of funding for the BBC's programming.

As a bureaucracy it enjoyed a great deal of autonomy in its decisions on what to broadcast. Full daytime television was not approved until the mid-1980s. The BBC has maintained admirable standards of excellence, impartiality and quality unaffected by commercial pressures.* With this freedom, the BBC produced children's programs, concerts, and other shows that were of cultural importance but would probably not survive in a wholly commercial environment. Radio sessions included performances by world-famous orchestras, but also by British and American pop music icons such as the Beatles, the Rolling Stones, Janis Joplin, Jimi Hendrix, and Chuck Berry. One of its most famous exports was the longest-running science-fiction series in the world, *Doctor Who*, which ran from 1963 until 1989.

Unfortunately, the BBC also suffered from some of the

---

*This led to another curious incident. In the 1980s, "Kodachrome," a song by Paul Simon (of Simon and Garfunkel fame), was banned from play by the BBC because it referred to a commercial product which, under BBC Charter and Licence, could not be broadcast.

same ills found in any other government agency. Any company with a fixed source of income must cut corners to stay within its budget and the confines of its facility. The BBC was no exception.

Early BBC programmes had been recorded on long-playing record, film and cinescope, maintained in the BBC Film Library. With the advent of commercial recording tape, another medium was added to the BBC archives. The corporation had a mandate to keep all programs on film, but no similar mandate was added to the charter to preserve video or audio tapes. Video tapes were under the auspice of the BBC Engineering Department until 1978, when the video library was at last merged with the film library. These tapes were kept in a smaller archive until they could be reviewed to see if they had any commercial potential for overseas sales. Many concerts and audio sessions were published and sold, as were numerous series, documentaries and movies, including *Doctor Who*, which, in the 1970s and 1980s, was one of the most-watched SF series in the world.

Space become a consideration, as did cost. So, sometime in 1967, some nameless bureaucrat decided to save both room and money by erasing audio and video tapes it had in storage, in order to reuse the tapes for new programs. Both the Film Library and the Engineering Department thought it was the other's responsibility to maintain historical copies of all programs. By 1978, when the policy was halted, so many programs were wiped out without any existing backup that the BBC had to appoint an Archive Selector to try to recover copies of programs from broadcast stations and collectors around the world. A very few of the missing treasures have been recovered. *Doctor Who* has a worldwide fan base that was able to

restore copies of several missing episodes to the BBC. Recently, two audio producers came forward to admit that
they defied the erasure order, and squirreled away copies
of unique sessions, including the earliest recording of the
Rolling Stones, called in to play backup for the legendary
Bo Diddley when British labor restrictions prevented his
backup musicians from obtaining work permits. These
"lost tapes" now have the potential to net the BBC a small
fortune, but it is a pittance compared with what is gone
for good.

As a result of trying to save a few pounds, thousands
of priceless gems of musical and broadcast history have
been lost. Each blank audio tape was reported to be worth
between £2.00 and £9.00. Not a large sum, considering
the millions of pounds the BBC might have earned on
publishing what had originally been recorded on them.
Among the lost recordings were early Beatles appearances, major dramatic presentations, news and historically
valuable footage, and historic sports events. The value
today can be estimated in the billions. But a little shelf
space was saved and a few thousands saved by reusing
the tapes. So, at the time, for what little thought was expended on it, it seemed like an expedient solution.

SNOW JOB

How Not to Get Elected
1978 Chicago

By Jody Lynn Nye

Chicago has had a reputation for decades as "The City That Works," for its matter-of-fact grasp of getting business done, particularly on behalf of its citizens: street cleaning, garbage pickup, public works. In February 1978, Chicago was hit by a powerful snowstorm that tied up the city. The city's Snow Command was criticized for botching its handling of the aftermath of the storm. Michael A. Bilandic, who had taken over the mayor's office on the death of legendary mayor Richard J. Daley, was determined that Chicago would not be taken by surprise by the weather again.

In April of 1978, Bilandic commissioned Administrative Management Improvement Systems (AMIS) to create a plan to manage the snow. AMIS was run by a lawyer named Kenneth Sain, who had been an administrative assistant under Daley and Bilandic, then deputy mayor of Chicago until his resignation in early 1977. Sain announced that the city had chosen his firm, replacing Barton-Aschmann Associates, because of his long association with city government.

On the first of December up to thirteen inches of snow fell on Chicago. Another heavy snow followed, bringing the total to fifteen inches in some areas. Obviously not a moment too soon, AMIS presented its final report, a twenty-three-page document, in December 1978, for which the city paid $90,000. The report reputedly contained proposals for equipment purchases and policy changes that would streamline Snow Command function. Streets and lots were plowed, and everyone congratulated themselves on managing the situation.

More snow fell on New Year's Eve, nearly nine inches, and the city's problems began in earnest. Snow Command, under the direction of Emmitt Garrity, assistant general superintendent of the Streets and Sanitation Department, was criticized for waiting almost a week before beginning to move cars off the streets so they could be plowed, as outlined under the city plan. The operation was at last underway, when the second-biggest snowstorm in the city's history fell, beginning on the twelfth of January.

The *Chicago Tribune* headline on January 14, 1978, said simply, "BLIZZARD . . ." Over the course of three days, 20.7 inches of snow fell on the city of Chicago. Between the heavy snow, plummeting temperatures and driving winds up to fifty mph, the city was paralyzed. O'Hare International Airport closed down, and traffic came to a halt. Mayor Bilandic announced emergency measures, and called for drivers to remove their cars from city streets. He offered the use of school and park district parking lots as temporary shelters so the streets could be clear for plowing. The order was to be enforced by the police, who would ticket and tow any cars left in the right of way.

Unfortunately, of the 103 lots Bilandic offered, fewer than half were plowed and available to the public. Cars were buried under mounds of snow, and side streets were not plowed because city vehicles couldn't get through. Bilandic issued an apology, vowing to discipline the employees who had told him the lots were clear. Nor was there enough equipment to handle the overwhelming mass of snow on the streets. A plea went out to nearby states for snow-removal gear and the personnel to operate it. Responses came from as far away as Quebec, but once in Chicago, operators claimed that no use was made of them. They were collecting as much as $57 per hour for doing nothing.

Unable to drive to work, people turned to public transportation. The bus system was no better than driving. Most streets were reduced to single lanes of traffic. Bus schedules were thrown off by as much as three hours, where service existed at all. Elevated trains ran, but undependably, continually falling prey to: derailments, as the compressed snow and ice thrust tracks out of alignment, causing many to crack; burned-out engines that disabled as many as a third of the available cars; snow-clogged brakes; and the addition of as much as 20 percent more ridership, from people who would otherwise drive. Two of the smaller urban train systems were put temporarily out of commission by four-foot drifts of snow that settled on the rails. No plows were available to clear the tracks, particularly the electrical third rail that provided motive power to the trains. It seemed that the last two track plows that the Chicago Transit Authority possessed had been taken out of service the previous year because the equipment that drove them was obsolete, and it was not considered necessary to replace them. In the end, one of the small lines made two plows out of plywood and strapped them to a train car to clear the rails.

By the time the snow slowed down, seventy-one inches had fallen on Chicago. Elderly people were trapped in their houses. Many were injured trying to carve paths in the snow so they could walk. Garbage pickup was suspended. By the thirty-first, most of the inner-city neighborhoods still had not been plowed. Bilandic announced the establishment of a snow help line, but it had only one number for all 5.5 million people in Chicago to call. The city seemed to have no direction in handling the blizzard, in spite of the much-touted snow plan the mayor had commissioned. Throughout it all, Mayor Bilandic made frequent television and radio appearances to assure the people that all that could be done was being done. The first letters to the editor were published calling for the mayor to resign over the mishandling of the snow emergency.

By January 19, there was a public outcry to see the Sain plan. Reluctantly, city hall released it to the press. Sain's allegedly fabulous snow plan turned out to be twenty-three pages of scanty outline, consisting of ridiculously simple instructions, such as telling employees to obey their supervisors and keep in touch with Snow Command at city hall, and instructions on how to fill out necessary forms. It included 184 maps of salting and plowing routes, but aldermen in the City Council claimed those were made up by city employees, not Sain. Nor did the report mention use of municipal lots for parking. Nor were there recommendations in the text for new equipment purchases, which had begun before AMIS was hired.

The most damning accusation came from a snow worker named Anthony Mazza, who claimed that the material in the report was lifted outright from the master's thesis he wrote in 1973 for his degree in Public Administration at Roosevelt University. The whole report was deemed a fraud, and efforts were made by the City Council to stop payments to Kenneth Sain. It was then that revelations began to surface that this was not the only contract that Sain had signed with Mayor Bilandic. The second was for a report to update the Police Department's Bomb and Arson squad. The third was for an examination of the Police and Fire Departments' 911 system. In all, Sain had garnered nine contracts with the city for a total of $242,000. The resulting scandal embarrassed Bilandic, causing him to lose credibility. His opponent in the February Democratic mayoral primary, Jane Byrne, had only to mention the weather snafu of two weeks earlier, to trounce him decisively for the nomination.

It seemed that the only truly effective snow job perpetrated in the City of Chicago in 1978 was the one that Sain and Company pulled on Mayor Michael Bilandic.

ONE HOUR TOO SHORT?

The 100 Hour War
1990 Persian Gulf

by Bill Fawcett

It is dangerous to second-guess anything recent as a mistake. History has a habit of changing your perspective over time. Many Americans praised the seeming stability and national spirit that the election of Adolf Hitler as chancellor of Germany brought about. Others felt avidly that Joseph McCarthy was saving the nation, while today we see he was actively undermining the Constitution.

Even though less than a decade has passed since the Gulf War, it is now apparent that there was one military decision made by then-president Bush which contrasts with all of the others he made. Among his best decisions was the one to allow the generals to actually run the war, unlike Lyndon Johnson who all but ordered the individual air strikes personally during Vietnam. President Bush's other great accomplishment was gathering a consensus for the military that included even the surrounding Arab nations. This also led to his one bad decision, that we are visibly and expensively paying for today.

After months of sitting on the borders of Iraq and Kuwait, the forces of the United Nations, the majority American military units and all under American command, began their invasion. After months of pounding from the air, the bulk of Iraq's army, mostly conscripts, was quickly scattered or captured. All seemed well.

But while the Arab allies wanted to make sure Sadam Hussein was no longer a threat to them, they had another concern. Based on realpolitik and racial awareness they were adamant that there not be a United Nations—read American—occupation of a major Arab country. After decades of American favoritism to Israel and the slow intervention by the U.S. and Europe in the Serbian slaughter of Islamic residents in the Balkans, most Arab leaders had what they felt was more than good cause to distrust the prejudices of the United States.

By the third day of the war it was apparent that the Iraqis had lost. The Republican Guard, which had most of their modern armor, had been slaughtered in the "mother of all battles" with little loss to the U.N. attackers. Kuwait had been completely reoccupied. The air defenses around Baghdad had been shown to be ineffective for months. The roads to Baghdad were crowded with retreating soldiers and Iraqi civilians. There was no longer even a single intact Iraqi military unit of any size between the U.S. armored divisions and Baghdad.

A further complication brought on by success was the position of much of the rest of the world, and particularly the Russian Confederation of States. These governments were adamant that the U.S. stick with its mandate from the U.N. to free Kuwait. The United Nations resolutions never spoke to replacing the Iraqi government or to what to do with Sadam Hussein himself, even though Bush had sought American support for the war by delaring "Sadam" the next Hitler, someone who had to be stopped at any cost. Had the U.S. continued to pursue the retreating Iraqi army, they were technically moving beyond what was called for by the Security Council resolutions on the war.

But beyond all the international considerations, there was one more. The past decades have shown that there is an element present in Arab culture, as well as others, that creates fanatics. This has been true since Islam first appeared, and remains true today. The United States, had it continued into Iraq, would have had no choice but to become the occupying power. Sadam Hussein had effectively eliminated any other political forces in his country years before. There was no one to take over an Iraqi government should we wish to replace Sadam's with another one. The incredible valor and nationalistic fervor shown by the Iraqi Army in its several years of warfare with Iran a few years earlier had demonstrated very clearly the determination of the people themselves.

Further, after Vietnam, the United States has become very aware of the difficulty in controlling even very low-tech insurrections in third-world countries. The high-tech weaponry and elite forces that crushed the half million man Iraqi army would have been less than effective in controlling a resentful population that harbored thousands of men who were willing to die to deliver a bomb to a café or barracks, a scenario that we have seen repeated in other places and for other reasons many times since the Gulf War ended.

So perhaps that is why President Bush left Sadam Hussein in control of his shattered nation. We simply weren't going to be able to control it if we did take the nation over. The difference between taking and holding was something the Soviet government found out about in nearby Afghanistan. Or maybe it was international pressure. All of our Arab allies were concerned about the U.S. establishing a precedent of replacing hostile Arab governments. Or maybe it was simply the appeal of ending the war with minimal casualties and in exactly 100 hours. Whatever the reason, the decision was made by President Bush to stop the offensive and leave Sadam Hussein in power.

Since then there have been several escalations, evidence the Iraqis are continuing to invest in biological and nuclear weapons, and ten times more money spent on our continued military presence in the Gulf than has been spent in the space program. The next decade or two will allow history to judge whether this was all such a good idea.

Index

About the Editors

William R. Forstchen is a professor of history at Montreat College in Black Mountain, NC. He is the author of more than fifteen books, both fiction and nonfiction.

Bill Fawcett has authored and edited more than a dozen books. He is also an Associate Publisher for Emperor's Press, an historical hardcover house.